Mary Elizabeth K. Bernhard

September 1993

Amherst

THE

MOTHER'S BOOK.

BY MRS. CHILD,

AUTHOR OF 'THE FRUGAL HOUSEWIFE,' 'THE GIRL'S OWN BOOK,'
'EVENINGS IN NEW ENGLAND,' AND EDITOR OF
'THE JUVENILE MISCELLANY.

The child is father of the man;
And I could wish his days to be
Bound each to each by natural piety.
Wordsworth.

Do you ask, then, what will educate your son? Your example will educate
him; your conversation; the business he sees you transact; the likings and
dislikings you express,—these will educate him—the society you live in will
educate him. *Mrs. Barbauld.*

Published in Cooperation with

Old Sturbridge Village

APPLEWOOD BOOKS

DISTRIBUTED BY THE GLOBE PEQUOT PRESS

The Mother's Book was originally published in 1831.

ISBN: 1-55709-124-2

10 9 8 7 6 5 4 3

Library of Congress Cataloging in Publication Data
Child, Lydia Maria Francis, 1802-1880
  The Mother's Book / by L. Maria Child.
    p.   cm.
  Originally published: Boston: Carter and Hendee, 1831.
  ISBN: 1-55709-124-2 : $9.95
  1. Child rearing. 2. Mother and child. 3. Children–
Conduct of life. I. Title.
HQ769.C4478   1992
649'.1–dc20   92-17577
                                                  CIP

TO

AMERICAN MOTHERS,

ON

WHOSE INTELLIGENCE AND DISCRETION

THE

SAFETY AND PROSPERITY

OF OUR

REPUBLIC SO MUCH DEPEND,

This Volume

IS

RESPECTFULLY INSCRIBED.

PREFACE.

When I wrote the 'Frugal Housewife,' some booksellers declined publishing it, on account of the great variety of cookery books already in the market. I was perfectly aware of this circumstance; but among them all, I did not know of one suited to the wants of the middling class in our own country. I believed such a book was needed; and the sale of more than six thousand copies in one year has proved that I was right in my conjecture.

If the same remark is made with regard to adding another to the numerous books on education, I have the same answer to give— I do not know of one adapted to popular use in this country.

I make no pretensions to great originality. The leading principles contained in this little volume have already been advanced in the

1 *

standard works on education; and I owe a
great deal to frequent conversations with an
intelligent and judicious mother. Perhaps
some will think there is egotism and pre-
sumption in the frequent repetition of '*I*
think,' and '*I* believe,' and 'It is *my* opinion'
—but it must be remembered that this could
not well be avoided in a work where familiarity and directness of expression were particularly required.

I have endeavored to give the result of
my own reading and observation in maxims
of plain practical good-sense, written with
earnestness and simplicity of style. How
far I have succeeded must be decided by
my readers.

INTRODUCTION.

———

I CANNOT offer a better or more appropriate introduction to this work, than an extract from Mr. Francis' Discourse on Errors in Education.

'It is not easy to estimate the influence even of what may seem an inconsiderable effort, when directed to such an object as education. It has been said, that a stone thrown into the sea agitates more or less every drop in that vast expanse of waters So it may be with the influence we exert on the minds and hearts of the young. Who can tell what may be the effects of a single good principle deeply fixed, a single pure and virtuous association strongly riveted, a single happy turn effectually given to the thoughts and affections? It may spread a salutary and sacred influence over the whole life and through the whole mass of the character of the child. Nay, more, as the characters of others, who are to come after him, may, and probably will, depend much on his, the impulse we give may not cease in him who first received it: it may go down from one generation to another, widening and deepening its influences as it goes, reaching forth with various modifications, more or less direct, till the track of its agency shall be completely beyond human calculation.'

'We are told, that when Antipater demanded of the Lacedemonians fifty of their children as hostages, they replied that they would rather surrender fifty of the most eminent men in the state, whose principles were already formed, than children to whom the want of early instruction would be a loss altogether irreparable. The Spartans were wise; and shall Christians be less so? Oh no;—for we believe that our labor cannot perish even with life;— we believe that, even if the inscrutable providence of God removes these objects of affection from us, neither the pleasure they have poured into our hearts, nor the good we have imparted to them will, or can, be lost.'

CONTENTS.

THE MOTHER'S BOOK.

CHAPTER I.

THE BODILY SENSES.

Few people think that the management of very young babes has anything to do with their future dispositions and characters; yet I believe it has more influence than can easily be calculated. One writer on education even ventures to say, that the heaviness of the Dutch and the vivacity of the French are owing to the different manner in which infants are treated in those two countries.

The Dutch keep their children in a state of repose, always rocking, or jogging them; the French are perpetually tossing them about, and showing them lively tricks. I think a medium between these two extremes would be the most favorable to a child's health and faculties.

An infant is, for a while, totally ignorant of the use of the senses with which he is endowed. At first, he does not see objects; and when he sees them, he does not know that he can touch them. 'He is obliged to serve an apprenticeship to the five senses,' and at every step he needs assistance in learning his trade. Any one can see that assistance tends to quicken the faculties, by observing how much faster a babe improves, when daily surrounded by little brothers and sisters.

But in trying to excite an infant's attention, care should be taken not to confuse and distract him. His soul, like his body, is weak, and requires to have but little sustenance at a time, and to have it often. Gentleness, patience, and love, are almost everything in education; especially to those helpless little creatures, who have just entered into a world where everything is new and strange to them. Gentleness is a sort of mild atmosphere; and it enters into a child's soul, like the sunshine into the rose-bud, slowly but surely expanding it into beauty and vigor.

All loud noises and violent motions should be avoided. They pain an infant's senses, and distract his faculties. I have seen impatient nurses thrust a glaring candle before the eyes of a fretful babe, or drum violently on the table, or rock the cradle like an earthquake. These things may stop a child's cries for a short time, because the pain they occasion his senses, draws his attention from the pain which first induced him to cry; but they do not comfort or soothe him. As soon as he recovers from the distraction they have occasioned, he will probably cry again, and even louder than before. Besides the pain given to his mind, violent measures are dangerous to the bodily senses. Deafness and weakness of eye-sight may no doubt often be attributed to such causes as I have mentioned; and physicians are agreed that the dropsy on the brain is frequently produced by violent rocking.

Unless a child's cries are occasioned by sharp bodily pain, they may usually be pacified by some pleasing object, such as stroking a kitten, or patting the dog; and if their tears are really occasioned by acute pain, is it not cruel to add another suffering, by stunning them with noise, or blinding them with light?

Attention should be early aroused by presenting attractive objects—things of bright and beautiful colors, but not glaring—and sounds pleasant and soft to the ear. When you have succeeded in attracting a babe's attention to any object, it is well to let him examine it just as long as he chooses. Every time he turns it over, drops it, and takes it up again, he adds something to the little stock of his scanty experience. When his powers of attention are wearied, he will soon enough show it by his actions. A multitude of new playthings, crowded upon him one after another, only serve to confuse him. He does not learn as much, because he does not have time to get acquainted with the properties of any one of them. Having had his little mind excited by a new object, he should be left in quiet, to toss, and turn, and jingle it, to his heart's content. If he look up in the midst of his play, a smile should be always ready for him, that he may feel protected and happy in the atmosphere of love.

It is important that children, even when babes, should never be spectators of anger, or any evil passion. They come to us from heaven, with their little souls full of innocence and peace; and, as far as possible, a mother's influence should not interfere with the influence of angels.

The first and most important thing, in order to effect this is, that the mother should keep her own spirit in

2

tranquillity and purity; for it is beyond all doubt that
the state of a mother affects her child. There are
proofs that it is true, both with regard to mind and body.
A mere babe will grieve and sob at the expression of
distress on a mother's countenance; he cannot possibly
know what that expression means, but he *feels* that it
is something painful—his mother's state affects him.

Effects on the bodily constitution will be more readily
believed than effects on the mind, because the most
thoughtless can see the one, and they cannot *see* the
other. Children have died in convulsions, in consequence of nursing a mother, while under the influence
of violent passion or emotion; and who can tell how
much of *moral* evil may be traced to the states of mind
indulged by a mother, while tending the precious little
being, who receives everything from her?

Therefore the first rule, and the most important of
all, in education, is, that a mother govern her own feelings, and keep her heart and conscience pure.

The next most important thing appears to me to be,
that a mother, as far as other duties will permit, take
the entire care of her own child. I am aware that
people of moderate fortune cannot attend exclusively to
an infant. Other cares claim a share of attention, and
sisters, or domestics, must be intrusted; but where this
must necessarily be the case, the infant should, as much
as possible, feel its mother's guardianship. If in the
same room, a smile, or a look of fondness, should now
and then be bestowed upon him; and if in an adjoining
room, some of the endearing appellations to which he
has been accustomed, should once in a while meet his
ear. The knowledge that his natural protector and

best friend is near, will give him a feeling of safety and protection alike conducive to his happiness and beneficial to his temper.

You may say, perhaps, that a mother's instinct teaches fondness, and there is no need of urging that point; but the difficulty is, mothers are sometimes fond by fits and starts—they follow impulse, not principle. Perhaps the cares of the world vex or discourage you—and you do not, as usual, smile upon your babe when he looks up earnestly in your face,—or you are a little impatient at his fretfulness. Those who know your inquietudes may easily excuse this; but what does the innocent being before you know of care and trouble? And why should you distract his pure nature by the evils you have received from a vexatious world? It does you no good, and it injures him.

Do you say it is impossible always to govern one's feelings? There is one method, a never-failing one—prayer. It consoles and strengthens the wounded heart, and tranquillizes the most stormy passions. You will say, perhaps, that you have not leisure to pray every time your temper is provoked, or your heart is grieved.—It requires no time—the inward ejaculation of 'Lord, help me to overcome this temptation,' may be made in any place and amid any employments; and if uttered in humble sincerity, the voice that said to the raging waters, 'Peace! Be still!' will restore quiet to your troubled soul.

As the first step in education, I have recommended gentle, but constant efforts to attract the attention, and improve the bodily senses. I would here suggest the importance of preserving the organs of those senses in

full vigor.   For instance, the cradle should be so placed
that the face of the infant may be in shade.   A
stream of light is dangerous to his delicate organs of
vision; and if it be allowed to come in at one side, he
may turn his eyes, in the effort to watch it.   Glaring
red curtains and brilliantly striped Venetian carpeting
are bad things in a nursery, for similar reasons.

I have said nothing concerning the physical wants of
children,—their food, diseases, &c,—because such subjects are not embraced in the design of the present work.

The judicious and experienced are universally agreed
that the best books for these purposes are, 'DEWEES'
TREATISE UPON CHILDREN,' and 'ADVICE TO YOUNG
MOTHERS, BY A GRANDMOTHER.'

CHAP. II.

THE AFFECTIONS.

THE cultivation of the affections comes next to the
development of the bodily senses; or rather they may
be said to begin together, so early does the infant heart
receive impressions.   The uniform gentleness, to which
I have before alluded, and the calm state of the mother's
own feelings, have much to do with the affections of the
child.

Kindness toward animals is of great importance.
Children should be encouraged in pitying their distress;

and if guilty of any violent treatment toward them, they should see that you are grieved and displeased at such conduct.

Before showing any disapprobation of his conduct, however, it should be explained to a very young child when he really does hurt an animal; for young children are often cruel from the mere thoughtlessness of frolic; they strike an animal as they would strike a log of wood, without knowing that they occasion pain.

I once saw a mother laugh very heartily at the distressed face of a kitten, which a child of two years old was pulling backward by the tail. At last, the kitten, in self-defence, turned and scratched the boy. He screamed, and his mother ran to him, kissed the wound, and beat the poor kitten, saying all the time, 'Naughty kitten, to scratch John! I'll beat her for scratching John! There, ugly puss!'

This little incident, trifling as it seems, no doubt had important effects on the character of the child; especially as a mother, who would do such a thing once, would be very likely to do it habitually.

In the first place, the child was encouraged in cruelty, by seeing that it gave his mother amusement. Had she explained to him that he was hurting the kitten, and expressed her pity by saying, 'Oh, don't hurt kitty—she is a good little puss—and she loves John'— what a different impression would have been made on his infant heart!

In the next place, the kitten was struck for defending herself; this was injustice to the injured animal, and a lesson of tyranny to the boy. In the third place, striking the kitten because she had scratched him, was teach-

2*

ing him retaliation.   For that reason, a chair or a foot-
stool, against which he had accidentally hurt himself,
should never be struck, or treated in an angry manner.
You know, to be sure, that an inanimate object is not
capable of feeling pain; but your infant does not know
it; the influence upon *him* is, that it is right to injure
when we are injured.

It is a common opinion that a spirit of revenge is
natural to children.   No doubt bad temper, as well as
other evils, moral and physical, are often hereditary—
and here is a fresh reason for being good ourselves, if
we would have our children good.   But allowing that
evil propensities are hereditary, and therefore born with
children, how are they excited, and called into action?

First, by the influences of the nursery—those early
influences, which, beginning as they do with life itself,
are easily mistaken for the operations of nature; and
in the second place, by the temptations of the world.

Now, if a child has ever so bad propensities, if the
influences of the nursery be pure and holy, his evils
will never be excited, or roused into action, until his
understanding is enlightened, and his principles formed,
so that he has power to resist them.   The temptations
of the world will then do him no harm; he will 'overcome evil with good.'

But if, on the other hand, the influences of the nursery are bad, the weak passions of the child are
strengthened before his understanding is made strong;
he gets into habits of evil before he is capable of perceiving that they are evil.   Consequently, when he
comes out into the world, he brings no armor against
its temptations.   Evil is within and without.   And

should the Lord finally bring him out of Egypt, it must be after a dark, and weary bondage.

The mind of a child is not like that of a grown person, too full and too busy to observe everything; it is a vessel empty and pure—always ready to receive, and always receiving.

Every look, every movement, every expression, does something toward forming the character of the little heir to immortal life.

Do you regard it as too much trouble thus to keep watch over yourself? Surely the indulgence of evil is no privilege: the yoke of goodness is far lighter and easier to bear, than the bondage of evil. Is not the restraint you impose upon yourself for the good of your child, blessed, doubly blessed, to your own soul? Does not the little cherub in this way guide you to heaven, marking the pathway by the flowers he scatters as he goes.

The rule, then, for developing good affections in a child is, that he never be allowed to see or feel the influence of bad passions, even in the most trifling things; and in order to effect this, you must drive evil passions out of your own heart. Nothing can be real that has not its home *within* us. The only sure way, as well as the easiest, to *appear* good, is to *be* good.

It is not possible to indulge anger, or any other wrong feeling, and conceal it entirely. If not expressed in words, a child *feels* the baneful influence. Evil enters into his soul, as the imperceptible atmosphere he breathes enters into his lungs: and the beautiful little image of God is removed farther and farther from his home in heaven.

CHAP. III.

INTELLECT.—ATTENTION.

THE first effort of intellect is to associate the names of objects with the sight of them. To assist a babe in this particular, when you direct his attention to any object, speak the name of the object, slowly and distinctly. After a few times, he will know the thing by its name; and if you say DOG, when the dog is not in the room, he will show that he knows what you mean, by looking round in search of him.

By degrees, a few words can be added. He will soon learn to repeat, 'Good little dog;' and though he may not have very exact ideas of what good means, the tone of the voice, and the manner in which you speak, will make him think it is something pleasant. When you draw a child's attention to a living thing, it is well to accompany it with some endearment to the animal; this will awaken his affections, as well as his thoughts. In teaching a child to talk, low, mild tones should be used.

Too much cannot be said on the importance of giving children early habits of observation. This must be done by teaching them to pay attention to surrounding objects, and to inquire the why and wherefore of everything. No doubt many mothers will say, 'I cannot thus train the minds of my children; for it is my misfortune not to have had an education myself.' This answer is very frequently given; and if by education is meant book-learning, the excuse is indeed a poor one. Good judgment, kind feelings, and habitual command over one's own passions, are necessary in the education of children; but learning is not necessary. The mother, who has had no other advantages than are furnished by a public school in a remote country village, knows a great many more things than a child of three or four years can possibly know. Early accustom your children to inquire about the things they handle. What if you cannot always answer them? You do them an immense deal of good by giving their minds active habits. If a spirit of inquiry is once aroused, it will, sooner or later, find means to satisfy itself; and thus the inquisitive boy will become an energetic, capable man.

I will give some familiar instances of what I mean. Generally speaking, when mothers have done superintending domestic concerns for the day, and have seated themselves, to 'take some comfort,' as the phrase is, 'with their children,' they spend the time in trotting them, or shaking the rattle, or dragging about the little cart, or repeating over and over again, 'pat a cake, pat a cake.' Now this is extremely well; and should on no account be omitted. But something ought to be mixed with these plays to give the child habits of thought. Toys amuse him for the time; but he grows weary of them, and when he does not hear, or see them, they do not furnish anything for him to think about. But should you, while tossing a ball, stop and say, 'This ball is *round;* this little tea-table is *square.* Now George knows what *round* and *square* mean,'—it would give him something to think about. When he has a new toy, he will think to himself whether it is round or

square.   It is not well to tell him more than one thing
at a time, or to enter into any detailed explanations.
It is a bad thing to have infant attention wearied. It
is enough for him to know that the ball is round and
the table square.   When he is older, you can explain to
him that a square has always equal sides, and that the
edge of a round thing is always equally distant from the
centre.

Another day, should you show him your ball of yarn,
and ask him if it be round or square, the chance is, he
will answer correctly. If he does recollect what you
have told him, it will make his little heart very happy;
and should you reward his answer with a smile and a
kiss, you will undoubtedly have done much to awaken
his powers of observation.

So much for the first step.—At another time, should
you chance to be spinning a dollar, or a cent, for his
amusement, you can, in the midst of the play, stop and
say, 'This dollar is round, as well as the ball; but the
dollar is flat, and the ball is not flat. If George puts
his hand on the dollar, he will feel that it is flat; and if
he puts his hand on the ball, he will feel that it is not
flat.   Now George knows what *flat* means.' Here I
would remark, that if the child is impatient to have the
dollar spinning, and does not love to hear about its
form, it is unwise to cross his inclinations. We never
remember so well what we do not love to hear; and
forced instruction is apt to injure the temper, and give
an early aversion to knowledge.

We are apt to forget that things long familiar to us
are entirely unknown to an infant. There is hardly
anything connected with his little wants, which may not

be made a pleasant medium of instruction. When eating a piece of bread, the following questions may be ˌasked and answered. 'What is bread made of?' 'I don't know; what is it made of, mother?' 'It is made of grain; sometimes of rye, sometimes of Indian meal, and sometimes of flour.' 'What is grain made of?' 'It grows in the field. The farmers plant it in the ground, and God causes it to grow.'

When a child is playing with his kitten, it is easy to mix instruction with his enjoyment, by saying, 'Feel pussy's fur—how smooth it is. Feel this piece of coral—how rough it is. Pussy's fur is smooth, and the coral is rough. Now George knows what *smooth* and *rough* mean.'

As he grows older, the information given him may be of a higher character. He can be told, 'The andirons are made of brass. Brass is called a metal; it is dug out of the earth.' At another time, he may be asked, 'What is the cover of your book made of?' If he answer, 'Of leather,' ask him what leather is made of. If he does not know, tell him it is made of a calf's skin Then ask him whether the cover of his book is a metal. If he say, 'No,' ask him what is the reason it is not. If he cannot answer, tell him, 'Because metals are always dug out of the earth. Leather is not dug out of the earth; it is made of calf-skin; therefore it is an *animal* substance, not a metal. Does George know what an animal is? It is a creature that grows, and can move about from one place to another. Your kitten is an animal; she grows bigger every day; and she moves about. The brass andirons are not animals. They do not grow any larger, and they cannot move.' Afterward,

when a proper opportunity occurs, ask him to tell you
the difference between a metal and an animal.

If he bring you a rose, you can say, 'Thank you,
George, for this rose. Now, can you tell me what it is?
Is it a metal?' 'No.' 'Is it an animal?' 'I should
think not, mother.' 'What is it, then?' 'I don't know.'
'I will tell you. It is a vegetable. Vegetables grow
out of the earth. They are not like metals, because
they grow larger and larger; and they are not like
animals, because they cannot move of themselves.
What are you, George?' 'I am not a metal, for I
grow bigger every day. I am not a vegetable, for I
can walk. I think I am an animal.' 'Right, my dear
son. Now you know the meaning of metals, animals,
and vegetables.'

Such conversations as these will make his thoughts
busy; and when he takes a book he will probably ask,
'What are the leaves of books made of?' 'They are
made of paper.' 'What is paper made of?' 'Of rags.'
'What are rags made of?' 'Sometimes of linen, and
sometimes of cotton. Cotton grows in a pod, and linen
is made from a plant called flax.' 'Then the leaves of
my book are vegetable.' This discovery, simple as it
is, will afford the boy great pleasure, and will make it
more easy to exercise his powers of thought.

I dare say the preceding hints will sound silly enough
to many mothers; but they are nevertheless founded in
reason and sound sense. It is a fact that children, thus
early accustomed to observe, will have a wonderful
power of amusing themselves. They will examine
every figure in the carpet. and think to themselves
whether it is round, or square; and will sit, by the half

hour, quietly watching the figures on copper-plate, or calico.

Arithmetic may very early be made a source of amusement; for children can very soon learn to count sticks or marbles, and tell how many they should have left, if you should take away any given number.

With regard to the kind of information conveyed, as well as the quantity, that should depend upon the child's age, intelligence, and progress; things which no person can have an opportunity to observe and know, so well as a mother. The system of making *use* of all the common incidents of life to convey knowledge, and improve the heart, may be begun in the earliest childhood, and continued even until youth ripens into manhood. I will give a simple instance: Quite a large boy, when sailing in a boat, may be asked to observe how the hills and the trees *seem* to move from him, while in fact the boat alone is moving. The simple fact may not be of much consequence to him; for if he is a bright boy, he would have noticed it himself, without being asked to attend to it: but you can make it the means of illustrating another idea, by saying, 'Just so the sun *seems* to move round the earth; but it does not move. The sun stands still, as the hills and trees do; but the earth is moving all the time.'

I am aware that these habits of inquiry are at times very troublesome; for no one, however patient, can be always ready to answer the multitude of questions a child is disposed to ask. But it must be remembered that all good things are accompanied with inconveniences. The care of children requires a great many sacrifices, and a great deal of self-denial; but the woman,

3

who is not willing to sacrifice a good deal in such a cause, does not deserve to be a mother. Besides, the thoughtless, indolent parent, who is not willing to make sacrifices, and take trouble, does in fact have the most trouble; for the evils she would not check at first, when it might easily have been done, afterward grow too strong for her management.

But to return to the subject of asking questions. It is a spirit which should not be discouraged; but at the same time, children should be taught that they cannot *always* be attended to. If you are otherwise occupied, and their inquiries distract you, think a moment, and collect yourself, lest you should answer pettishly.

Do not say, ' How you plague me, Jane ! I wish you would go away, and keep still!' But say, ' I am very busy now, Jane. I cannot attend to you. If you will remember to ask me by and by, when I can attend to you, I will talk with you about it.' If the child persists, the answer should be, ' You know I always tell you what you ask, when I am not very busy. I cannot attend to you now ; and if you teaze me, I shall be very sorry; for I shall be obliged to put you out of the room.' After this threat is once made, nothing should induce you to refrain from observing it. In order that your child may be easily satisfied with these kind, but firm refusals, when you are busy, you should try to bear in mind the question she has asked, and take the first leisure moment to reply to it. This will give her confidence in what you have said; and she will know it was not done merely to put her off.

Perhaps another difficulty may occur; your children may ask questions that you do not know how to answer

In that case, as in all others, the honest truth should be told. The reply should be, 'I do not know. When father comes home, we will ask him; perhaps he can tell us.' If father does not know, the answer should be, 'As soon as you have money enough, I will buy you a book, that will tell all about it:' and this, like all other things that are promised, should be done.

If, as is often the case, a child asks an explanation, which would be altogether above his powers of comprehension, the answer should be, 'If I were to tell you, you could not understand it now.' You must wait till you are older.' If your child has been early accustomed to the strictest regard to truth, he will believe what you say, and try to be satisfied. Some children, being too much praised for their quickness, or their wit, ask a number of useless, pert questions. This disposition should be promptly and decidedly checked; for it is the germ of vanity and affectation. To avoid exciting this evil in the mind of a bright child, a very intelligent question, or remark, should never be quoted as anything remarkable, nor should he be at all encouraged to show off before company. The habit of reciting verses, and displaying other acquirements before strangers, seems to me the worst of all possible things for children. They should be taught to love knowledge for the sake of the good it will enable them to do others, not because they will gain praise by it. An inordinate love of reputation is always a powerful temptation to active minds; and the more the evil is fostered in the nursery, the harder it is to overcome. Children should hear learning, and wealth, and all other external gifts,

spoken of according to their true value—that is, their
usefulness. They should be told, 'The more knowledge you gain, the more useful you can be, when you
become a man.'

Perhaps you will say, that as your children grow
older, they cannot help learning that a rose is a vegetable, the andirons a metal, &c.; and you will ask what is
the use of teaching it to them a few years earlier than
they would naturally take to find it out of themselves. I
readily allow that the knowledge itself is of very little
consequence to them; but the *habits of attention and
activity of mind*, which you give them, are worth everything.

If you take the trouble to observe, you will find those
who are the most useful, and of course the most successful, in any department, are those who are in the
habit of observing closely, and thinking about what
they observe.

Why is it that a botanist will see hundreds of plants
in a field, which the careless stroller may pass again and
again without perceiving? It is because his *attention*
has been fixed upon plants. How is the great novelist
enabled to give you such natural pictures of life and
manners? A close *attention* to all the varieties of human character, enables him to represent them as they
are.

You will find that a smart, notable housewife is always an '*observing* woman.' What constitutes the
difference between a neat, faithful domestic, and a heedless, sluttish one? One pays *attention* to what she is
about, and the other does not. The slut's hands may
be very dirty, but she does not *observe* it; every time

she takes hold of the door, she may leave it covered with black prints, but she does not *observe* it. One educated to *attend* to things about her, would immediately see these defects and remedy them.

We often hear it said, ' Such a person has good sense, and good feelings; but, somehow or other, he has no faculty.' The ' faculty' that is wanting is nothing more or less than active habits of observation acquired in early life.

Those who give their attention exclusively to one thing, become great in that one thing; and will in all probability be careless and unobserving about everything else. This sort of character is not desirable; for if it makes a man greater in one particular branch, it much impairs his general usefulness. In a woman it is peculiarly unfortunate; for, whether she be rich or poor, the sphere allotted her by Providence requires attention to many things.

Literary women are not usually domestic; not because they cannot easily be so—but because they early acquired the habit of attending to literary things, and of neglecting others. It is not true that intellectual pursuits leave no time to attend to the common concerns of life. A fashionable woman spends more time and thought about her dress, than the most learned woman spends about books. It is merely *attention* that is wanted to make the belle literary, and the learned lady domestic.

All the faculties of a child's mind should be cultivated, and they should early acquire a power of varying their attention, so as to be able to bestow it easily upon any subject whatsoever. Some think it a sign of good

3 *

sense to despise good taste; hence the universal complaint that scholars are awkward and slovenly. Unquestionably this is better than the silly pursuit of ever-varying fashion; but there is no need of either extreme—extremes always lie on one side or the other of truth and nature.

Some, seeing the disastrous effects of an over-heated imagination, think that any degree of imagination is inconsistent with good judgment. This is a mistake.—The finest imagination may be kept perfectly in check by good sense, provided all the powers of the mind are *equally* cultivated in early life. A great writer has said, 'In forming the human character, we must not proceed as a statuary does in forming a statue, who works sometimes on the face, sometimes on the limbs, and sometimes on the folds of the drapery; but we must proceed (and it certainly is in our power) as nature does in forming a flower, or any other of her productions; she throws out altogether and at once the whole system of being, and the rudiments of all the parts.'

To a woman, the power of changing attention is peculiarly valuable. I have said that an exclusive attention to learning was a fault, as well as an exclusive attention to fashion; but while I condemn the *excessive* love of books, I must insist that the power of finding enjoyment in reading is above all price, particularly to a woman. A full mind is a great safeguard to virtue and happiness in every situation of life. Multitudes of people do wrong from mere emptiness of mind, and want of occupation.

Children should be early taught by example to listen

attentively to intelligent conversation, and should afterward be encouraged in referring to it. This will occasion a thirst for information, which will lead to a love of reading. But while you try to encourage a love of books, remember to direct their attention to other things at the same time. For instance, show your daughter at which end you begin to grate a nutmeg, and explain to her that if you began at the end once fastened to the branch, it would grate full of holes; because the fibres which held it together were fastened at that place, and being broken, they fall out. When sewing, you can call attention to the fact that sewing-silk splits much better for being first drawn through the wax; and that a wristband is put on before the sleeve is sewed, because it can be managed more conveniently.

I mention these merely as familiar instances how the attention may be kept awake, and ready to devote itself to little things, as well as great. If a girl feels interested in nothing but books, she will in all probability be useless, or nearly so, in all the relations dearest to a good woman's heart; if, on the other hand, she gives all her attention to household matters, she will become a mere drudge, and will lose many valuable sources of enjoyment and usefulness. This may be said in favor of an over-earnest love of knowledge—a great mind can attend to little things, but a little mind cannot attend to great things.

CHAP. IV.

MANAGEMENT.

THIS phrase is a very broad and comprehensive one. Under it I mean to include all that relates to rewards and punishments, and the adaptation of education to different characters and dispositions.

The good old fashioned maxim that 'example is better than precept,' is the best thing to begin with. The great difficulty in education is that we give *rules* instead of inspiring *sentiments*. The simple fact that your child never saw you angry, that your voice is always gentle, and the expression of your face always kind, is worth a thousand times more than all the rules you can give him about not beating his dog, pinching his brother, &c. It is in vain to load the understanding with rules, if the affections are not pure. In the first place, it is not possible to make rules enough to apply to all manner of cases; and if it were possible, a child would soon forget them. But if you inspire him with right *feelings*, they will govern his *actions*. All our thoughts and actions come from our affections; if we love what is good, we shall think and do what is good. Children are not so much influenced by what we say and do in particular reference to them, as by the general effect of our characters and conversation. They are in a great degree creatures of imitation. If they see a mother fond of finery, they become fond of finery; if they see her selfish, it makes them selfish; if they see her extremely anxious for the attention of wealthy people, they learn to think wealth is the only good.

Those whose early influence is what it should be, will find their children easy to manage, as they grow older.

An infant's wants should be attended to without waiting for him to cry. At first, a babe cries merely from a sensation of suffering—because food, warmth, or other comforts necessary to his young existence, are withheld; but when he finds crying is the only means of attracting attention, he soon gets in the habit of crying for everything. To avoid this, his wants should be attended to, whether he demand it or not. Food, sleep, and necessary comforts should be supplied to him at such times as the experience of his mother may dictate. If he has been sitting on the floor, playing quietly by himself a good while, take him up and amuse him, if you can spare time, without waiting for weariness to render him fretful. Who can blame a child for fretting and screaming, if experience has taught him that he cannot get his wants attended to in any other manner?

Young children should never be made to cry by plaguing them, for the sake of fun; it makes them seriously unhappy for the time, and has an injurious effect upon their dispositions. When in any little trouble, they should be helped as quick as possible. When their feet are caught in the rounds of a chair, or their playthings entangled, or when any other of the thousand-and-one afflictions of baby-hood occur, it is an easy thing to teach them to wait by saying, ' Stop a minute, and I will come to you.' But do not say this, to put them off; attend to them as quick as your employments

will permit; they will then wait patiently should another disaster occur. Children, who have entire confidence that the simple truth is always spoken to them,
are rarely troublesome.

A silent influence, which they do not perceive, is
better for young children than direct rules and prohibitions. For instance, should a child be in ill humor,
without any apparent cause, (as will sometimes happen)
—should he push down his playthings, and then cry
because he has injured them—chase the kitten, and
then cry because she has run out of his reach—it is
injurious to take any direct notice of it, by saying, 'How
cross you are to-day, James! What a naughty boy
you are! I don't love you to-day.' This, in all probability, will make matters worse. The better way is
to draw off his attention to pleasant thoughts by saying,
'I am going in the garden'—or, 'I am going out to see
the calf. Does James want to go with me?' If, in
the capriciousness of his humor, he says he does not
want to go, do not urge him : make preparations to go,
and he will soon be inclined to follow. A few flowers,
or a little pleasant talk about the calf, will, in all probability, produce entire forgetfulness of his troubles. If
the employment suggested to him combine usefulness
with pleasure,—such as feeding the chickens, shelling
peas for dinner, &c., so much the better. The habit of
assisting others, excites the benevolent affections, and
lays the foundation of industry.

When a little child has been playing, and perhaps
quarrelling, out of doors, and comes in with his face all
of a blaze, sobbing and crying, it is an excellent plan
to take him by the hand and say, 'What is the matter,

my dear boy? Tell me what is the matter. But, how dirty your face is! Let me wash your face nicely, and wipe it dry, and then you shall sit in my lap and tell me all about it.' If he is washed gently, the sensation will be pleasant and refreshing, and by the time the operation is finished, his attention will be drawn off from his vexations; his temper will be cooled, as well as his face. Then seat him in your lap, encourage him to tell you all about his troubles, comb his hair gently in the mean time, and in a few minutes the vexation of his little spirit will be entirely soothed. This secret of calling off the attention by little kind offices is very valuable to those who have the care of invalids, or young children. Bathing the hands and feet, or combing the hair gently, will sometimes put a sick person asleep when he can obtain rest in no other way.

An experienced and very judicious mother told me that, in the course of twenty years' experience, she had never known washing the face and combing the hair, fail to soothe an angry and tired child. But then it must be done gently. The reason children frequently have an aversion to being washed is that they are taken hold of roughly, and rubbed very hard. If you occasion them pain by the operation, can you wonder they dread it?

By such expedients as I have mentioned, ill-humor and discontent are driven away by the influence of kindness and cheerfulness; ' evil is overcome with good.' Whipping and scolding could not have produced quiet so soon; and if they could, the child's temper would have been injured in the process.

I have said that example and silent influence were

better than direct rules and commands. Nevertheless, there are cases where rules must be made; and children must be taught to obey implicitly. For instance, a child must be expressly forbidden to play with fire, to climb upon the tables, &c. But whenever it is possible, restraint should be invisible.

The first and most important step in management is, that whatever a mother says, always *must* be done. For this reason, do not require too much; and on no account allow your child to do at one time, what you have forbidden him at another. Sometimes when a woman feels easy and good-natured, and does not expect any company, she will allow her children to go to the table and take lumps of sugar; but should visiters be in the room, or she out of humor with the occurrences of the day, she will perhaps scold, or strike them, for the self-same trick. How can a mother expect obedience to commands so selfish and capricious? What inferences will a child draw from such conduct? You may smile at the idea that very young children draw inferences; but it is a fact, that they do draw inferences —and very just ones too. We mistake, when we trust too much to children's not thinking, or observing. They are shrewd reasoners in all cases where their little interests are concerned. They know a mother's ruling passion; they soon discover her weak side, and learn how to attack it most successfully. I will relate a little anecdote, to show that children are acute observers of character. A wealthy lady, fond of dress and equipage, was the mother of a thoughtless little rogue. One day, he seized hold of a demijohn of wine, which a larger boy had placed upon the side-walk of a secluded alley, while he joined his companions in play; the little fellow persisted in striking the demijohn on the pavement, for his amusement. He was repeatedly warned that he would break the bottle and spill the wine; and at last this did happen. His mother, being told of the mischief he had so wantonly done, immediately paid for the wine, and ordered him to be undressed and put to bed, although it was then in the middle of the day. While this operation was performed by the nursery maid, he said, 'Betsy, it is my private opinion, that I should have had a whipping *if mother hadn't had her best gown on.*'*

To return to my subject.—The necessity of obedience early instilled is the foundation of all good management. If children see you governed by a real wish for their good, rather than by your own selfishness, or capricious freaks, they will easily acquire this excellent habit. Wilful disobedience should never go unpunished. If a little child disobeys you from mere forgetfulness and frolic, it is best to take no notice of it; for his intention is not bad, and authority has greater effect when used sparingly, and on few occasions. Should he forget the same injunction again, look at him very seriously, and tell him that if he forgets it again, you shall be obliged to punish him. Should he commit the offence the third time, take from him the means of committing it; for instance, if you tell him not to tear his picture-book, and he does tear it, take it away from him. Perhaps he will pout and show ill humor;—will push off with his little chair, and say, 'I don't love you, mother.' —If so, take no notice. Do not laugh, for that would

---

* It is but justice to this boy to state, that he was prompt in confessing his fault, and eager to atone for it.

4

irritate him, without performing the least use; do not seem offended with him, for that will awaken a love of power in his little mind. It excites very bad feelings in a child to see that he can vex a parent, and make her lose her self-command. In spite of his displeasure, therefore, continue your employment tranquilly, as if nothing had happened. If his ill humor continue, however, and show itself in annoyances to you, and others around him, you should take him by the hand, look very seriously in his face, and say, 'James, you are such a naughty boy, that I must punish you. I am very sorry to punish you; but I must, that you may remember to be good next time.' This should be done with perfect calmness, and a look of regret. When a child is punished in anger, he learns to consider it a species of revenge; when he is punished in sorrow, he believes that it is done for his good.

The punishment for such peevishness as I have mentioned should be being tied in an arm-chair, or something of that simple nature. I do not approve of shutting the little offender in the closet. The sudden transition from light to darkness affects him with an undefined species of horror, even if he has been kept perfectly free from frightful stories. A very young child will become quite cold in a few minutes, at midsummer, if shut in a dark closet.

If the culprit is obstinate, and tries to seem as if he did not care for his punishment, let him remain in confinement till he gets very tired; but in the meanwhile be perfectly calm yourself, and follow your usual occupations. You can judge by his actions, and the expression of his countenance, whether his feelings begin to soften. Seize a favorable moment, and ask him if he is sorry he has been so naughty; if he says, 'Yes,' let him throw himself into your arms, kiss him, and tell him you hope he will never be naughty again; for if he is you must punish him, and it makes you very sorry to punish him. Here is the key to all good management: always punish a child for wilfully disobeying you in the most trifling particular; but never punish him in anger.

I once heard a lady very pertly say, 'Well, I should be ashamed of myself if I *could* punish a child when I was not angry. Anybody must be very hard-hearted that can do it.' Several of her companions laughed at this speech; but for myself, I saw neither wit nor wisdom in it.

The woman who punishes her child because she is angry, acts from the selfish motive of indulging her own bad passions; she who punishes because it is necessary for the child's good, acts from a disinterested regard to his future happiness.

As for the kind and degree of punishment, it should be varied according to the age and character of the child, and according to the nature of the offence. We must remember that very young children do not know what is right and wrong, until we explain it to them. A child should not be punished the first time he tears his picture-book, or cuts his gown. He should be told that it is very naughty, and that he must not do it again. It is well to show the torn book to his father, and other members of the family, saying with a look of concern, ' See how George has torn his picture-book! What a pity. I am *so* sorry.' This will impress the magnitude of the fault upon his mind, and he will not be so likely to forget it.

But should he make a grieved lip, and appear distressed at your conversation, change the current of his feelings by saying, 'But I am sure he will never do such a naughty thing again. He is sorry for it.' Having thus impressed his mind, do not recur to the subject again.

The form of punishment should always be as mild as it can be and produce the desired effect. Being sent to bed in the middle of the day is a great privation; and it does not excite bad feelings so much as some other forms of punishment. Small children may be tied in an arm-chair, sent out of the room and forbidden to return, put to bed without supper, &c. Eating dinner separate from the family, or not being allowed to kiss father and mother, is a grievous penance to children of sensibility. Privation of any expected pleasure usually makes a deep impression.

Where it is possible, it is a good plan to make the punishment similar to the offence. If a child is quarrelsome, or mischievous, among his companions, make him play in a room by himself. If he is studying with others, and chooses to be very disobliging, or annoying, send him to another room to study alone ; or, if this is not convenient, make him sit at a table by himself, and allow no one to speak to him during the evening. His offences having been anti-social, his punishment should be so likewise. Being deprived of social intercourse will teach him its value.

If a child abuse any good thing, it is well to take it from him, and make him feel the want of it,

Thus if he abuse your confidence, do not trust him again for some time.   But if he is really repentant, restore it to him; and when you do trust him, trust him entirely.   Allusions to former faults have a disheartening effect, particularly on sensitive, affectionate children.

Above all things, never suffer a child to be accused of a fault, until you are perfectly sure he has been guilty of it.   If he is innocent, the idea that you could think him capable of wickedness will distress him, and will in some degree weaken the strength of his virtue.   I would rather lose the Pitt diamond, if it were mine, than let an innocent child know he had been for one moment suspected of stealing it.   The conscious dignity of integrity should always be respected.

While speaking of punishments, I would suggest one caution.   Never undertake to make a child do a thing unless you are very sure you can make him do it.   One instance of successful resistance to parental authority will undo the effects of a year's obedience.   If a boy is too bad to be governed by any other means than flogging, and is too strong for you, do not attempt to manage him : tell his father, or his guardians, of his disobedience, and request them to punish him.

Fear should on no occasion be used as a preventive, or a punishment.   If children want anything improper for them to have, do not tell them it will bite them.   It is not true ; and the smallest child will soon learn by experience that it is not true.   This will teach him to disbelieve you, when you really do tell the truth, and will soon make a liar of him.   Care should be taken not to inspire a terror of animals, such as beetles, mice, spiders, &c.   Fortunately we have no venomous creatures in

4 *

New-England, which are likely to infest the nursery.
As for spiders, they are quite as likely to bite a child
who is afraid of them, as one who is not; and if such a
thing should happen, a little swelling, and a few hours'
pain, are not half as bad as fear, that troubles one all
his life long. Children would never have fear of
animals, unless it were put into their heads. A little
girl of my acquaintance once came running in with a
striped snake, exclaiming ' Oh, what a beautiful creature
I have found !' Her mother acknowledged that she
shuddered, because she had herself been taught to fear
snakes; but she knew the creature would not hurt her
daughter, and she would not allow herself to express
any horror; she merely advised her to set the animal
at liberty.

Not to kill any animal, seems to me an excess of a
good thing. The vermin that infest our houses and
gardens must be destroyed, and children must see them
destroyed. But it should always be done with expressed regret, and as mercifully as possible. The explanation that we kill them to prevent the evil they would
do, is very good, and very satisfactory. But the fact is,
there are very few creatures in this climate which do us
harm; more than half our aversions to animals are mere
prejudices.

However, it is not evils which can be seen, met, and
understood, that usually frighten children. A child is
told that fire will burn him if he touches it, and if he
has been accustomed to the truth, he believes it; but
he will stay in the room where there is a fire without
fear; for he knows by experience, that the fire cannot
come to him. But they are frightened with mysterious.

ideas of something in the dark—with stories of old men prowling about to steal them—rats and mice that will come and bite them, when they are shut up in the closet, &c.

I cannot find language strong enough to express what a woman deserves, who embitters the whole existence of her offspring by filling their minds with such terrific images. She who can tell a frightful story to her child, or allow one to be told, ought to have a guardian appointed over herself.

Let us examine what the motives must be, that lead to such measures. It is indolence—pure indolence; a mother is not willing to take the pains, and practise the self-denial, which firm and gentle management requires; she therefore terrifies her child into obedience. She implants in his mind a principle that will, in all probability, make him more or less wretched through his whole life, merely to save herself a few moments' trouble! Very strong minds may overcome, or nearly overcome, early impressions of this kind; but in cases of weak nerves, or acute natural sensibility, it is utterly impossible to calculate the extent of the evil. And all this to save a little trouble! What selfishness!

However, Divine Providence has so ordered it, that whatever is wrong, is really bad *policy*, as well as bad *morality*. 'Lazy people *must* take the most pains' in the end. Fill your children with fears to make them obedient, and those very fears become your tyrants. They cannot go into the dark without you; and you must sit by their bedside till sleep relieves them from terror. All this is the consequence of avoiding a little trouble in the beginning. Is it not a dear price for the whistle?

The management of children should vary according
to their character.   A very active mind, full of restless
curiosity, does not need to be excited; but a feeble or
sluggish character should be aroused, as much as possible, by external means.   For instance, if there is any
wonderful sight to be seen in the neighborhood, such as
a caravan of animals, a striking picture, wonderful mechanism, &c., and if it be inconvenient for you to take
more than one of the children under your care, let the
treat be given to the one whose character most needs to
be aroused.   Of course, I do not mean that *lazy* children should be entertained, in preference to industrious
ones; I mean where there is a pre-disposition to dul-
ness, owing to early disease, an afflicted state of his
mother's mind before his birth, or while nursing him,
&c;—in such cases, the thoughts and affections should
be excited with an extraordinary degree of care.   A
timid child should be encouraged more than a bold and
confident one; and if necessary to punish him, means
should be used as little likely to break his spirit as possible.   A boy whose perceptions are slow, and who
learns with labor and difficulty, should be indulged in
reading a new book, or attending to a new branch of
study, which particularly interests him; but a boy of
quick perceptions, and ready memory, should be kept
at one thing as long as possible.   Such different characters are in danger of totally different defects.   One
is in danger of never getting his mind interested in
knowledge, and the other of getting so much interested
in everything, that he will learn nothing well; therefore they should be managed in a manner entirely
opposite.

The same rule holds good with regard to the affections : cultivate most those faculties and good feelings, which appear to be of the slowest growth. If a love of power early develope itself in one member of your family with more strength than in the others, subject that child to more restraint than you do the others. But in checking him, do not yourself act from a love of power : explain to him, at every step, that you govern him thus strictly, only to assist him in overcoming a great evil. If you really act from this motive, your child will perceive it to be true, and will respect you.

There is such an immense variety in human character, that it is impossible to give rules adapted to all cases. The above hints will explain my general meaning ; and observation and experience will enable a judicious mother to apply them with wisdom and kindness. I will merely add to what I have said, the old proverb, that ' An ounce of prevention is worth a pound of cure.'—If a child has any evil particularly strong, it is far better to avoid exciting it, than to punish it when it is excited. Whatever may be the consequences of evil, it always gains fresh power over us by every instance of indulgence. As much as possible, keep a young child out of the way of temptation which it is peculiarly hard for him to resist; and by reading, by conversation, by caresses, make him in love with the opposite good ; when once his *feelings* are right on the subject, temptation will do him good instead of harm.

When a child is to be punished, he should always be told calmly, ' I am obliged to do this for your good. If I do not punish you, you will not remember next time. You have promised two or three times to do as I bade you, but you always forget it; now I must make you suffer a little, that you may remember it.'

A very young child can understand and appreciate this management. I knew a girl of five years old, who had the habit of biting her nails so close, that her fingers were perpetually inflamed. Her mother had tried arguments, and various privations, without producing much effect. One day, the child, as usual, put her fingers to her mouth, to bite her nails; but suddenly withdrawing them, she came up to her mother's writing table, and said, 'Mother, slap my hand smartly with your ruler every time I bite my nails, and then I shall remember.' Her mother did as she was desired, saying, 'I hope you will remember now, and that I shall never have to do this again.' The girl winced a little, —for her mother did slap her smartly, though but a very few times; but she seemed perfectly satisfied, and said, 'I think that will make me remember it.' For several days afterward, if she moved her fingers to her mouth, she would look at the writing table and smile; and if her mother perceived her, she would hold up her finger in a cautioning manner, and smile also. All this was done in perfect good-nature on both sides. After a while she forgot herself, and bit her nails again; her mother was not in the room; but she went, of her own accord, and avowed the fact, saying, 'Mother, give me a few more slaps than you did before; and see if that will make me remember it any longer.' After that, she never needed correction for the same fault This little girl understood the real *use* of punishment; she did not look upon it as a sign of anger, but as a means of helping her to overcome what was wrong.

Mere fear of suffering never makes people really better. It makes them *conceal* what is evil, but it does not make them *conquer* it. They must be taught to dislike what is wrong merely because it is wrong, and to look upon punishment as a means to help them to get rid of it. Does sickness, and misery, and ruin deter the vicious from the commission of sin? Is not theft indulged at the very foot of the gallows? If a man do not hate what is wrong, the mere fear of consequences will never cleanse his heart, though it may regulate his outward behavior; and what will mere outward goodness avail him in another world, where there is no possibility of concealment, or hypocrisy? What the child is, the man will probably be; therefore never make the avoidance of punishment a *reason* for avoiding sin.

Having mentioned that a mother slapped her little girl smartly, I shall very naturally be asked if I approve of whipping. I certainly do not approve of its very frequent use; still I am not prepared to say that it is not the best punishment for some dispositions, and in some particular cases. I do not believe that most children, properly brought up from the very cradle, would need whipping; but children are not often thus brought up; and you may have those placed under your care in whom evil feelings have become very strong. I think whipping should be resorted to only when the same wrong thing has been done over and over again, and when gentler punishments have failed. A few smart slaps sometimes do good when nothing else will; but particular care should be taken not to correct in anger.

Punishments which make a child ashamed should be avoided. A sense of degradation is not healthy for the character. It is a very bad plan for children to be brought into a room before strangers with a foolscap, or some bad name, fastened upon them. Indeed, I think strangers should have as little as possible to do with the education of children; to be either praised, or mortified, before company, makes us care too much about the opinion of others. I do not mean to inculcate a defiance of public opinion; such contempt springs from no good feeling, and like all wrong things, is neither becoming, nor expedient. The approbation of others does make us happy, and there is no reason why it should not; but when we do right *because* people will approve of it, we begin at the wrong end. If we follow conscientiously what we perceive to be good, we shall be certain never to be misled; but if we do what others think right, we shall follow a very uncertain guide, and pollute the best of actions with a wrong motive. Nay, worse than all, we shall gradually lose the perception of what is right; and if folly and sin are the fashion, we shall first *feel* that they are fascinating, and then begin to *reason* openly (when we dare) that there is no harm in them.

Nothing is a safe guide but the honest convictions of our own hearts. A good man *will* always be respected; but he cannot be really good *because* he shall be respected for it. Indeed those who have been taught no holier motive than that of gaining the good opinion of others, rarely succeed in permanently keeping what they covet so much. The *heart* is not right; and however clean they may try to keep the outside, at some unlucky moment hypocrisy will fail them, and their real character will peep through.

You may tell a cross, discontented looking woman that the world would like her face a great deal better, if it were cheerful and benevolent; but how is she to alter the expression of her face? The mere selfish wish to be pleasing will not enable her to do it. She must begin with her *heart*, and religiously drive from thence all unkind and discontented feelings.

What a change would take place in the world if men were always governed by internal principle! If they would make pure the hidden fountain, the light might shine upon the wandering stream, and find it clear and stainless in all its windings!

I have heard parents say to children, 'If you don't get your lessons better, you will grow up a dunce, and *everybody will laugh at you*.' The thing to which they are urged is good, but the motive is wrong. If young people are taught to regulate their actions by a dread of the world's laugh, they will be full as likely to be deterred from good, as from evil. It would be much better to say, 'If you grow up in ignorance, you cannot *do half as much good* in the world, as you can if you gain all the knowledge in your power. Now, while you are young, is the best time to fit yourself for being useful.'

I once heard a boy say, 'Well, mother, I got a grand ride to-day. Last week I told a man one of his wagon wheels was coming off; and when I was walking home from school to-day, the same man overtook me, and asked me to get in and ride. You always told me, *if I helped others, they would help me*.' This is a common case. Parents are in the habit of telling children, 'If you will be good, you will *lose nothing by it*.' This is poisoning the act in the motive. It is not true

5

that we always meet a return for kindness and generosity; they who expect it will be disappointed; and not being accustomed to act from any better motive, they will cease to be benevolent, except when they are sure of reward. We should look for the recompense of goodness in our own hearts; there we shall certainly find it. The reward is *in* keeping the commandments, not *for* keeping them.

Children should be induced to kindness by such motives as the following: ' God is very good to us, and ought we not to be so to others? The Bible tells us to do to others as we would be done by; and you know very well how pleasant it is when you are in trouble to have other people pity you and help you. When you do good to others, does it not make you very happy?'

People sometimes double a boy's lesson because he has not behaved well. This is a very bad plan. If his book is used as a punishment, how can you expect him to love it? For the same reason, never tell a child he shall stay at home from school if he is good; this gives him the idea that going to school is a task. On the contrary, make all his associations with school as pleasant as possible. Speak of the kindness of the instructer in taking so much pains to teach him; encourage him in telling you about what he has learned; show pleasure at the progress he makes; and tell him how useful he will be when he is a man, if he continues so industrious and persevering.

Never offer money as a reward for doing right. Money and praise become necessary if once habituated to them; so much so, that it is impossible to act without some selfish excitement. Money is the worst stimulus

of the two; for avarice is more contemptible and injurious in its effects than a too earnest desire for the good
opinion of others.

At the same time guard against wastefulness and
prodigality. Teach children to be very economical—
never to cut up good pieces of calico, or paper, for no
purpose—never to tear old picture-books, destroy old
playthings, burn twine, or spend every cent they receive
for cake and sugar-plums. But as a reason for not
destroying, tell them these things will come in *use*.
Encourage them in laying up money to buy an orange
for a sick neighbor, a pair of shoes for a poor boy, or a
present to surprise his sister on her birth-day—anything,
—no matter what,—that is not for himself alone. He
will thus learn the value of money, without becoming
selfish. To avoid the danger of engrafting avarice upon
habits of care, earnestly encourage children to be generous
in giving and lending to each other; and show peculiar
delight when they voluntarily share anything of which
they are particularly fond. If a child has in any way
acquired a tendency to parsimony, take extraordinary
pains to make him feel happy when he has been
generous. Praise him even more than you would think
safe under any other circumstances; for it is always
prudent to assist a child most in those points where he
is the weakest. To be sure, your approbation is not
the best motive he might have; but it is better than the
hope of public applause; and moreover it is the best
motive from which he *can* act, until he gets rid of his
bad habit. Help him to overcome the obstacle which
habit has thrown in his way, and he will gradually learn
to love generosity for its own sake.

Habits of carelessness, such as leaving things lying about, blotting books, reciting in a jumbled manner, or jumping hastily at incorrect conclusions, &c., should be resolutely and promptly checked. Defects of this sort are the origin of numerous evils. Many a failure in business, many a disordered household, may be traced to the indulgence of these habits in early life. I speak feelingly on this subject; for years of self-education have hardly yet enabled me to cure the evil. I have made mistakes both in conversation and writing, concerning things which I knew perfectly well, merely from an early habit of heedlessness. It is has cost me much mortification and many tears; punishments which certainly have improved my habits, and may in time cure them.

No single instance of carelessness should be overlooked. If a little girl cannot find her gloves, or her bonnet, when you are about to take a walk, oblige her to stay at home. Let no tears and entreaties induce you to excuse it. I dare say, it may sometimes be painful to you to pursue this course; but for your child's sake, have resolution enough to do it.

If a boy loses his book, and cannot therefore get his lesson at the usual time, see that he is deprived of his play-hours in order to learn it. If he habitually forgets his book, send him back to the school-house for it, even if it be cold weather, and a great distance.

If a girl is always losing her thimble, do not lend her one; let her hurt her finger a little by sewing without one. These small cruelties in the beginning will save a great deal of future suffering. In order to leave no excuse for carelessness, children should be provided with a proper place for everything, and taught always to put it there, as soon as they have done using it.

Perhaps there is no evil into which children so easily and so universally fall as that of lying.

The temptation to it is strong, and therefore the encouragement to veracity should be proportionably strong. If a child breaks anything and honestly avows it, do not be angry with him. If candor procures a scolding, besides the strong effort it naturally costs, depend upon it, he will soon be discouraged. In such cases, do not speak till you can control yourself—say, 'I am glad you told me. It was a very valuable article, and I am truly sorry it is broken; but it would have grieved me much more to have had my son deceive me.' And having said this, do not reproachfully allude to the accident afterward. I was about to say that children should *never* be punished for what was honestly avowed; but perhaps there may be *some* cases where they will do again and again what they know to be wrong, from the idea that an avowal will excuse them; in this case, they tell the truth from policy, not from conscience; and they should be reasoned with, and punished. However, it is the safe side to forgive a good deal, rather than run any risk of fostering habits of deception. Should you at any time discover your child in a lie, treat it with great solemnity. Let him see that it grieves you, and strikes you with horror, as the worst of all possible faults. Do not restore him to your confidence and affection, until you see his heart is really touched by repentance. If falsehood becomes a habit with him, do not tempt him to make up stories, by asking him to detail all the circumstances connected with

5 *

the affair he has denied. Listen coldly to what he says, and let him see by your manner, that you do not ask him questions, because you have not the least confidence in his telling the truth. But remember to encourage, as well as discourage. Impress upon his mind that God will help him to get rid of the evil whenever he really wishes to get rid of it; and that every temptation he overcomes will make the next one more easy. Receive any evidence of his truth and integrity with delight and affection; let him see that your heart is full of joy that he has gained one victory over so great a fault.

Let your family never hear trifling deceptions glossed over by any excuses; speak of them with unlimited abhorrence and contempt.

Above all things, let your own habits be of the strictest truth. Examine closely! You will be surprised to find in how many little things we all act insincerely. I have at this moment in my memory a friend, who probably would be very indignant to be told she did not speak the truth; and I dare say, on all that she deemed important occasions, she might be relied on; yet she did deceive her children. True, she thought it was for their good; but that was a mistake of hers; deception never produces good. I one evening saw her remove a plate of plum-cake from the tea-table to the closet. Her youngest daughter asked for a piece; the reply was, ' It is all gone.—Puss came and ate it up ;' at the same time the mother winked to a little girl, two or three years older, not to *tell* that she had seen her put it in the closet. There is an old proverb about killing two birds with one stone—here two daughters were injured by one lie. The youngest was deceived, and the oldest was taught to participate in the deception. Mere experience would soon teach the little girl that the cat did not eat the cake; and having found that her mother would lie, she would in all probability dispute her even when she spoke the truth. And after all, what use is there in resorting to such degrading expedients? Why not tell the child, 'The plum-cake is in the closet; but it is not good for you at night, and I shall not give you a piece until morning?' If she had been properly educated, this would have satisfied her; and if she chose to be troublesome, being put to bed without her supper would teach her a lesson for the future.

A respect for the property of others must be taught children; for until they are instructed, they have very loose ideas upon the subject. A family of children cannot be too much urged and encouraged to be generous in lending and giving to each other; but they should be taught a scrupulous regard for each other's property. They should never use each other's things, without first asking, 'Brother, may I have your sled?' 'Sister, may I have your book?' &c. They should be taught to put them carefully in place, when they have done using them; and should be impressed with the idea that it is a greater fault to injure another's property, than to be careless of our own. If any little barter has been made, and a dispute afterwards arises, hear both sides with perfect impartiality, and allow no departure from what was promised in the bargain. From such little things as these, children receive their first ideas of honesty and justice.

Some children, from errors in early management, get

possessed with the idea that they may have everything.
They even tease for things it would be impossible to
give them. A child properly managed will seldom ask
twice for what you have once told him he should not
have. But if you have the care of one who has acquired this habit, the best way to cure him of it is never
to give him what he asks for, whether his request is
proper or not ; but at the same time be careful to give
him such things as he likes, (provided they are proper
for him,) when he does not ask for them. This will
soon break him of the habit of teasing.

I have said much in praise of gentleness. I cannot
say too much. Its effects are beyond calculation, both
on the affections and the understanding. The victims
of oppression and abuse are generally stupid, as well as
selfish and hard-hearted. How can we wonder at it?
They are all the time excited to evil passions, and nobody encourages what is good in them. We might as
well expect flowers to grow amid the cold and storms
of winter.

But gentleness, important as it is, is not all that is required in education. There should be united with it
firmness—great firmness. Commands should be rea-
sonable, and given in perfect kindness ; but once given,
it should be known that they must be obeyed. I heard
a lady once say, ' For my part, I cannot be so very
strict with my children. I love them too much to punish
them every time they disobey me.' I will relate a
scene which took place in her family. She had but one
domestic, and at the time to which I allude, she was
very busy preparing for company. Her children knew
by experience that when she was in a hurry she would

indulge them in anything for the sake of having them out of the way. George began, 'Mother, I want a piece of mince-pie.' The answer was, 'It is nearly bed-time; and mince-pie will hurt you. You shall have a piece of cake, if you will sit down and be still.' The boy ate his cake; and liking the system of being hired to sit still, he soon began again, 'Mother, I want a piece of mince-pie.' The old answer was repeated. The child stood his ground, 'Mother, I want a piece of mince-pie—I *want* a piece—I *want* a piece,' was repeated incessantly. 'Will you leave off teasing, if I give you a piece?' 'Yes, I will,—certain true.' A small piece was given, and soon devoured. With his mouth half full, he began again, 'I want another piece—I want another piece.' 'No, George; I shall not give you another mouthful. Go sit down, you naughty boy. You always act the worst when I am going to have company.' George continued his teasing; and at last said, 'If you don't give me another piece, I'll roar.' This threat not being attended to, he kept his word. Upon this, the mother seized him by the shoulder, shook him angrily, saying, 'Hold your tongue, you naughty boy!' 'I will if you will give me another piece of pie,' said he. Another small piece was given him, after he had promised that he certainly would not tease any more. As soon as he had eaten it, he, of course, began again; and with the additional threat, 'If you don't give me a piece, I will roar after the company comes, so loud that they can all hear me.' The end of all this was, that the boy had a sound whipping, was put to bed, and could not sleep all night, because the mince-pie made his stomach ache. What an accumulation of

evils in this little scene! His health injured,—his
promises broken with impunity,—his mother's promises
broken,—the knowledge gained that he could always
vex her when she was in a hurry,—and that he could
gain what he would by teasing. He always acted upon
the same plan afterward; for he only once in a while
(when he made his mother very angry) got a whipping;
but he was *always* sure to obtain what he asked for, if
he teased her long enough. His mother told him the
plain truth, when she said the mince-pie would hurt him;
but he did not know whether it was the truth, or whether she only said it to put him off; for he knew that she
did sometimes deceive. (She was the woman who
said the cat had eaten the cake.) When she gave him
the pie, he had reason to suppose it was not true it would
hurt him—else why should a kind mother give it to her
,child? Had she told him that if he asked a second
time, she should put him to bed directly—and had she
kept her promise, in spite of entreaties,—she would have
saved him a whipping, and herself a great deal of
unnecessary trouble. And who can calculate all the
whippings, and all the trouble, she would have spared
herself and him? I do not remember ever being in her
house half a day without witnessing some scene of con-
tention with the children.

Now let me introduce you to another acquaintance.
She was in precisely the same situation, having a comfortable income and one domestic; but her children
were much more numerous, and she had had very limit-
ed advantages for education. Yet she managed her
family better than any woman I ever saw, or ever expect to see again. I will relate a scene I witnessed

there, by way of contrast to the one I have just described. Myself and several friends once entered her parlor unexpectedly, just as the family were seated at the supper-table. A little girl, about four years old, was obliged to be removed, to make room for us. Her mother assured her she should have her supper in a very little while, if she was a good girl. The child cried; and the guests insisted that room should be made for her at table. 'No,' said the mother; 'I have told her she must wait; and if she cries, I shall be obliged to send her to bed. If she is a good little girl, she shall have her supper directly.' The child could not make up her mind to obey; and her mother led her out of the room, and gave orders that she should be put to bed without supper. When my friend returned, her husband said, 'Hannah, that was a hard case. The poor child lost her supper, and was agitated by the presence of strangers. I could hardly keep from taking her on my knee, and giving her some supper. Poor little thing! But I never will interfere with your management; and much as it went against my feelings, I entirely approve of what you have done.' 'It cost me a struggle,' replied his wife; 'but I know it is for the good of the child to be taught that I mean exactly what I say.'

This family was the most harmonious, affectionate, happy family I ever knew. The children were managed as easily as a flock of lambs. After a few unsuccessful attempts at disobedience, when very young, they give it up entirely; and always cheerfully acted from the conviction that their mother knew best. This family was governed with great strictness; firmness was united with gentleness. The indulgent mother, who said she loved her children too much to punish them, was actually obliged to punish them ten times as much as the strict mother did.

The husband's remark leads me to say something of the great importance of a perfect union between husband and wife. A want of this in education is like mildew in spring. A mother should never object to a father's punishing a child when he thinks proper; at least she should not do it before the child. Suggestions to each other may, of course, be made in all the freedom of mutual respect and affection. One parent should never allow a child to do what the other has forbidden; no expression of disapprobation concerning management should ever be made by either party, except when alone. A young child ought never to suspect it is possible for his parents to think differently concerning what relates to his education. Perhaps you will ask, if, after all I have said in praise of truth, I approve of concealment and deception in this particular. But you will please to recollect it is not *truth* which I advise to have concealed in this instance; it is only *a difference of opinion*. The child, not being old enough to understand the reasons why his parents differ, cannot receive any good from the discussion. Implicit obedience is the first law of childhood. The simple belief that their parents know what is best, is all the light children have to follow, at first. If they see their parents do not agree between themselves as to what is right, it naturally weakens their confidence, and makes them uncertain which they ought to obey. 'My dear, I don't approve of your management'—or, 'I should not have allowed him to do as you have done '—or, ' Your father may approve of it, but I don't '—are very improper and injurious expressions. If you differ in your ideas of education, take a proper opportunity to discuss the matter in freedom and kindness; but do not weaken the respect of your children by expressing doubts of each other's good judgment in their presence. It is hardly possible to exaggerate the bad effects of discord between parents; and the blessed influence of domestic union may well be compared to a band of guardian angels protecting innocence from all evil things.

If your marriage has been an unfortunate one—if the influence of a father may not be trusted—or if he delights in thwarting your well-meant endeavors—I know not what to say. If patience, humility and love cannot win him to a sense of duty, the only thing you can do, is to redouble your vigilance for the good of your children, and as far as possible withdraw them from his influence. Until it becomes an imperious duty, never speak of a parent's errors; unless there is great danger of their being imitated, let a thick veil rest upon them. But why should I dwell upon a case so unnatural, so wretched, and so hopeless? If such be your unhappy lot, pray to God, and he will give you light to make the path of duty clear before you. He alone can help you.

6

CHAP. V.

PLAYTHINGS.—AMUSEMENTS.—EMPLOYMENTS.

In infancy, the principal object is to find such toys as are at once attractive and safe. During the painful process of teething, a large ivory ring, or a dollar worn smooth, are good, on account of the ease they give the gums; they should be fastened to a string—but not a green one, or any other from which a babe can suck the colors. Some people think nothing so good for teeth-ing children as a large, round piece of India rubber, from which it is impossible to bite a piece. Painted toys are not wholesome at this age, when children are so prone to convey everything to the mouth. A bunch of keys is a favorite plaything with babies. Indeed any-thing they can move about, and cause to produce a noise, is pleasant to them. I have seen infants amuse themselves, for hours, with a string of very large wooden beads, or shining buttons; perhaps it is needless to say that no buttons but steel, wood, or ivory, are safe; if they have any portion of brass about them, they are injurious: another caution, perhaps equally unnecessary, is, that playthings small enough to be swallowed should be tied together with a very strong string, from which no color can be extracted. When children are a few months older, blocks of wood, which can be heaped up and knocked down at pleasure, become favorite play-things. A pack of old cards are perhaps liked still better, on account of their bright colors and pictured faces. Such toys are a great deal better than expensive ones. I do not think it a good plan to give children old almanacs, pamphlets, &c., to tear up. How can they distinguish between the value of one book and another? Children, who have been allowed to tear worthless books, may tear good ones, without the least idea that they are doing any harm.

As soon as it is possible to convey instruction by toys, it is well to choose such as will be useful. The letters of the alphabet on pieces of bone are excellent for this purpose. I have known a child of six years old teach a baby-brother to read quite well, merely by playing with his ivory letters. In all that relates to developing the intellect, very young children should not be hurried or made to attend unwillingly. When they are playing with their letters, and you are at leisure, take pains to tell them the name of each one, as often as they ask; but do not urge them. No matter if it takes them three weeks to learn one letter; they will not want their knowledge in a hurry. When the large letters are learned, give them the small ones. When both are mastered, place the letters together in some small word, such as CAT; point to the letters, name them, and pronounce *cat* distinctly. After a few lessons, the child will know what letters to place together in order to spell cat. Do not try to teach him a new word, until he is perfectly master of the old one; and do not try to force his attention to his letters, when he is weary, fretful and sleepy, or impatient to be doing something else. In this, as indeed in all other respects, an infant's progress is abundantly more rapid, if taught by a brother, or sister, nearly of his own age. The reason is, their little minds are in much the same state as their pupil's; they are therefore less liable than ourselves to miscalculate his strength, or force him beyond his speed. Among instructive toys may be ranked balls arranged together so as to be counted.

Every step of infantile progress should be encouraged by expressions of surprise and pleasure. When a child is able to spell a new word, or count a new number, kiss him, and show delight at his improvement. Sir Benjamin West relates that his mother kissed him eagerly, when he showed her a likeness he had sketched of his baby-sister; and he adds, '*That kiss made me a painter!*'

I have before shown that the same rule applies to the affections—that it is better to encourage what is right, than to punish what is wrong. Nothing strengthens a child in goodness, or enables him to overcome a fault, so much as seeing his efforts excite a sudden and earnest expression of love and joy.

For children of two or three years old, pictures are great sources of amusement and instruction. Engravings of animals on large cards are very good things. It is a great object to have proportion observed; if a child have a very small picture of an elephant, and a very large one of a mouse, it will lead him to the conclusion that a mouse is as large as an elephant. Children should be encouraged in talking about the engravings they look at; and the different parts should be pointed out and explained to them. Thus if a palm-tree is placed near the picture of an elephant, the attention should be drawn to it, and it should be explained to them that it is not the picture of any tree in this country, (that is, in New England,) but that in Asia and

Africa, where elephants live, palm-trees are very common. If a child is old enough to understand it, some account of this useful tree may be given advantageously; he can be told that it yields palm-oil, palm-wine, that its leaves are manufactured into fans, &c. But if he is not old enough to feel interested in such an account, do not trouble him with it. The object of pointing out all the details of an engraving, and explaining them, when they differ from what he is accustomed to see, is merely to give *habits of observation*, and arouse a spirit of inquiry.

I think it is very important that disproportioned, badly drawn pictures should not be placed in the hands of children. No matter how coarse or common they are, but let them be correct imitations of nature; if they are graceful, as well as correct, so much the better. Good taste is of less consequence than good feelings, good principles, and good sense; but it certainly is of consequence, and should not uselessly be perverted or destroyed. I believe the sort of pictures children are accustomed to see have an important effect in forming their taste. The very beggar-boys of Italy will observe a defect in the proportions of a statue, or a picture ; and the reason is, that fine sculpture and paintings are in their churches, and about their streets.

Playthings that children make for themselves are a great deal better than those which are bought for them. They employ them a much longer time, they exercise ingenuity, and they really please them more. A little girl had better fashion her cups and saucers of acorns, than to have a set of earthen ones supplied. A boy takes ten times more pleasure in a little wooden sled he

6 *

has pegged together, than he would in a painted and gilded carriage brought from the toy-shop; and I do not believe any expensive rocking-horse ever gave so much satisfaction, as I have seen a child in the country take with a long-necked squash, which he had bridled and placed on four sticks. There is a peculiar satisfaction in inventing things for one's self. No matter if the construction be clumsy and awkward; it employs time (which is a great object in childhood), and the pleasure the invention gives is the first impulse to ingenuity and skill. For this reason, the making of little boats, and mechanical toys, should not be discouraged; and when any difficulty occurs above the powers of a child, assistance should be cheerfully given. If the parents are able to explain the principles on which machines are constructed, the advantage will be tenfold.

Cutting figures in paper is a harmless and useful amusement for those who are old enough to be trusted with scissors; which, by the way, should always be blunt-pointed, when placed in the hands of a very young child. Any glaring disproportion in the figures should be explained to a child, and he should be encouraged to make his little imitations as much like nature as possible. There is at present a little boy in Boston, who at two years old took a great fancy to cutting figures in paper. In the course of six or eight years, he actually wore out five or six pairs of scissors in the service. He cuts with astonishing rapidity, and apparently without any thought; yet he will produce little landscapes, or groups, as beautiful and spirited as the best engravings. At first he began by copying things he had before him; but he afterward attained to so much skill,

that he easily invented his own designs. This talent has
enabled him to do a great deal for the support of his
parents, who are not rich.

Drawing figures on a slate is a favorite amusement
with children; and it may prove a very useful one, if
pains are taken to point out errors, and induce them to
make correct imitations. Young people should be taught
that it is not well to be careless in doing even the most
trifling things—that whatever is worthy of being done at
all, is worthy of being well done.

Some distinguished writers on education have ob-
jected to dolls, as playthings which lead to a love of
dress and finery. I do not consider them in this light.
If a mother's influence does not foster a love of finery,
I think there is very little danger of its being produced
by dressing dolls. I like these toys for various reasons.
They afford a quiet amusement; they exercise ingenuity
in cutting garments, and neatness in sewing; they can be
played with in a prodigious variety of ways; and so far
as they exercise the affections, their influence is innocent
and pleasant. No doubt dolls sometimes excite very
strong affection. Miss Hamilton tells of a little girl,
who had a limb amputated at the hospital. She bore the
operation with great fortitude, hugging her doll in her
arms all the time. When it was completed, the surgeon
playfully said, 'Now let me cut off your doll's leg.'
This speech produced a torrent of tears, and the little
creature could hardly be pacified. She had borne her
own sufferings patiently, but she could not endure that
her doll should be hurt. I know that this tenderness
for inanimate things is not the best employment for the
affections; but so far as it goes, it is good. For the

same reason, and in a similar degree, I think pet animals have a good effect; but care should be taken to choose such as are happy in a domesticated state. I cannot think it is right to keep creatures, that must be confined in cages and boxes; no pleasure can be good, which is so entirely selfish.

It is a benefit to children to have the care of feeding animals, such as lambs, chickens, &c. It answers two good purposes—it excites kindness, and a love of usefulness.

Amusements and employments which lead to exercise in the open air have greatly the advantage of all others. In this respect, I would make no difference between the management of boys and girls. Gardening, sliding, skating, and snow-balling, are all as good for girls as for boys. Are not health and cheerful spirits as necessary for one as the other? It is a universal remark that American women are less vigorous and rosy, than women of other climates; and that they are peculiarly subject to disorders of the chest and the spine. I believe the sole reason of this is, that our employments and amusements lead us so little into the open air.

I am aware that many people object to such plays as I have recommended to girls, from the idea that they will make them rude and noisy. I do not believe this would be the case if the influences within doors favored gentleness and politeness; and even if there were any danger of this sort, how much easier it is to acquire elegance in after life, than it is to regain health! When it is considered what a loss of usefulness, as well as comfort, is attendant upon ill health, I think all will agree that a vigorous constitution is the greatest of earthly blessings.

When I say that skating and sliding are proper amusements for girls, I do not, of course, mean that they should mix in a public crowd. Such sports, when girls unite in them, should be confined to the inmates of the house, and away from all possibility of contact with the rude and vicious. Under these circumstances, a girl's manners cannot be injured by such wholesome recreations. To snow-ball, or slide, with well-behaved brothers every day, cannot, I am sure, tend to make a girl rude and boisterous. I know one very striking instance of the truth of what I assert; and no doubt the memory of my readers will supply similar proofs. Mrs. John Adams, wife of the second President of the United States, and mother of the sixth, was very remarkable for the elegance and dignity of her manners. Even amid the splendor of foreign courts, she was considered a distinguished ornament. Yet Mrs. Adams had not been brought up in petted indolence, or shut from the sun and air, for fear of injury to her beauty, or her gracefulness. She was a capable, active, and *observing woman;* and while she was the admiration of European courts, she knew how to make butter and cheese as well as any woman in Weymouth, which was her native place. In the latter part of her life, she was one day passing the home of her childhood, in company with an intimate friend; she paused, and looked at a long lane near the house, saying in an animated tone, ' Oh, how many hours and hours I have driven hoop up and down that lane!' As might be expected, Mrs. Adams enjoyed a hale and happy old age. Among the other good effects of her example, she has left a practical lesson to her country-women, that refined elegance is perfectly compatible with driving hoop in the open air.

I cannot pass over the subject of amusements, without saying something in relation to children's balls and parties. I do not believe human ingenuity ever invented any thing worse for the health, heart, or happiness—any thing at once so poisonous to body and soul. I do not, of course, refer to a social intercourse between the children of different families—that should be encouraged. I mean regular parties, in imitation of high-life—where children eat confectionary, stay late, dress in finery, talk nonsense, and affect what they do not feel—just as their elders in the fashionable world do. It is a heart-sickening sight to see innocent creatures thus early trained to vanity and affectation. In mercy to your children, trust not their purity and peace in such a sickly and corrupting atmosphere. 'Who was your beau last night?' said a girl of eight years old to another of ten. 'I danced twice with George Wells,' was the reply. 'Did you wear your pink sash, or your blue one?' I could have wept in very pity for the guileless young creatures, into whose cup of life poison had been so early poured! I speak the more earnestly on this subject, because it has become so general a habit with all classes of people to indulge children in balls and parties.

As for dancing, within and of itself, I see no objection to it. It is a healthy, innocent, and graceful recreation. The vanity and dissipation, of which it has usually been the accompaniment, have brought it into disrepute with the conscientious. But if dancing be made to serve the purpose, which all accomplishments should serve,—

that of ministering to the pleasure of father, mother, brothers, sisters and friends,—it is certainly innocent and becoming. I do not mean to imply that it is wrong to dance anywhere else but at home.—I simply mean that girls should not learn an accomplishment for the *purpose* of display among strangers. Let them learn anything which your income allows (without a diminution of comfort or benevolence)—but teach them to acquire it as a means of future usefulness, as a pleasant resource, or for the sake of making home agreeable—not with the hope of exciting admiration abroad.

It is very important, and very difficult, to furnish young children with sufficient employment. What we call a natural love of mischief, is in fact nothing but activity. Children are restless for employment; they must have something to do; and if they are not furnished with what is useful or innocent, they will do mischief. No one who has not lived with a family of children can conceive how very difficult it is to keep a child of five or six years old employed. It is a good plan to teach little girls to knit, to weave bobbin, watchguards, chains, &c. Making patchwork is likewise a quiet amusement; and if a child be taught to fit it herself, it may be made really useful. If the corners are not fitted exactly, or the sewing done neatly, it should be taken to pieces and fitted again; for it is by inattention to these little things that habits of carelessness are formed. On no occasion whatever should a child be excused from finishing what she has begun. The custom of having half a dozen things on hand at once, should not be tolerated. Everything should be finished, and well finished. It ought to be considered a disgrace to give up anything, after it is

once undertaken.   Habits of perseverance are of incalculable importance; and a parent should earnestly improve the most trifling opportunities of impressing this
truth.   Even in so small a thing as untying a knot, a
boy should be taught to think it unmanly to be either
impatient or discouraged.

Always encourage a child in fitting her own work, and
arranging her own playthings.   Few things are more valuable, in this changing world, than the power of taking
care of ourselves.   It is a useful thing for children to
make a little shirt exactly after the model of a large one,
fitting all the parts themselves, after you have furnished
them with a model of each part in paper.   Knitting
may be learned still earlier than sewing.   I am sorry to
see this old fashioned accomplishment so universally dis-
carded.   It is a great resource to the aged; and women,
in all situations of life, have so many lonely hours, that
they cannot provide themselves with too many resources
in youth.   For this reason I would indulge girls in
learning anything that did not interfere with their duties,
provided I could afford it as well as not ; such as all
kinds of ornamental work, boxes, baskets, purses, &c.
Every new acquirement, however trifling, is an additional
resource against poverty and depression of spirits.

The disposition to help others should be cherished
as much as possible.   Even very little children are
happy when they think they are useful.   'I can do *some*
good, can't I, mother?' is one of the first questions asked.
To encourage this spirit, indulge children in assisting you, even when their exertions are full as much
trouble as profit.   Let them go out with their little bas-
ket, to weed the garden, to pick peas for dinner, to feed

the chickens, &c. It is true they will at first need constant overseeing, to prevent them from pulling up flowers as well as weeds; but then it employs them innocently, and makes them happy; and if dealt gently with, they soon learn to avoid mistakes. In the house, various things may be found to employ children. They may dust the chairs, and wipe the spoons, and teach a younger brother his lessons, &c. As far as possible keep children always employed—either sewing, or knitting, or reading, or playing, or studying, or walking. Do not let them form habits of listlessness and lounging. If they endeavor to assist you, and do mischief while they are really trying to do their best, do not scold at them; merely explain to them how they should have gone to work, and give them a lesson of carefulness in future.

As girls grow older, they should be taught to take the entire care of their own clothes, and of all the light and easy work necessary in their own apartments.

I have said less about boys, because it is not so difficult to find employment for them as for girls. The same general rules apply to both. Boys should be allowed to assist others, when they possibly can, and should be encouraged in all sorts of ingenious experiments not absolutely mischievous. In general it is a good rule to learn whatever we can, without interfering with our duties. My grand-mother used to say, 'Lay by all scraps and fragments, and they will be sure to come in use in seven years.' I would make the same remark with regard to scraps and fragments of knowledge. It is impossible for us to foresee in youth, what will be the circumstances of our after life; the kind of information, which at one period seems likely to be of very little use to us, may

7

become very important. If I happened to be thrown into the society of those who excelled in any particular branch, I would gain all the information I could, without being obtrusive. No matter whether it be poetry, or puddings,—making shoes, or making music,—riding a horse, or rearing a grape-vine ;—it is well to learn whatever comes in one's way, provided it does not interfere with the regular discharge of duty. It was a maxim with the great Sir William Jones, 'never to lose an opportunity of learning anything.'

CHAP. VI.

THE SABBATH.—RELIGION.

It is a great misfortune for people to imbibe, in the days of childhood, a dislike of the Sabbath, or a want of reverence for its sacred character. Some parents, from a conscientious wish to have the Sabbath kept holy, restrain children in the most natural and innocent expressions of gayety—if they laugh, or jump, or touch their play-things, they are told that it is wicked to do so, because it is Sunday.—The result of this excessive strictness is that the day becomes hateful to them. They learn to consider it a period of gloom and privation; and the Bible and the church become distasteful, because they are associated with it. A little girl of my acquaintance, in the innocence of her heart, once made an exclamation, which showed what she really thought of Sunday. She had long been very anxious to go to the theatre; and when she was about six or seven years old, her wish was very injudiciously gratified. The after-piece happened to be Der Freyschutz, a horrible German play, in which wizards, devils, and flames are the principal agents. The child's terror increased until her loud sobs made it necessary to carry her home. 'What is the matter with my darling? asked her grandmother —Don't she love to go to the theatre?' 'Oh, grandmother!' exclaimed the sobbing child, 'it is a great deal worse than going to meeting!' My motive in mentioning this anecdote will not, of course, be misunderstood. Nothing is farther from my intentions than to throw ridicule upon any place of worship. It is merely introduced to show that Sunday was so unpleasantly associated in the child's mind, as to make her involuntarily compare it with anything disagreeable or painful; being restrained at home every moment of the day, made the necessary restraint at church irksome to her; whereas with proper management it might have been a pleasant variety.

Some parents, on the other hand, go to the opposite extreme; and from the fear of making the Sabbath gloomy, they make no distinction between that and other days. This is the more dangerous extreme of the two. A reverence for the Sabbath, even if it be a mere matter of habit, and felt to be a restraint, is very much better than no feeling at all upon the subject. But it appears to me that a medium between the two extremes is both easy and expedient. Children under five or six years old cannot sit still and read all day; and being impossible, it should not be required of them. They may be made to look on a book, but they cannot be made to feel interested in it, hour after hour. Childhood is so restless, so active, and so gay, that such requirements will be felt and resisted as a state of bondage. Moreover, if a child is compelled to keep his eyes on a book, when he does not want to read, it will early give the impression that mere outward observances constitute religion. It is so much easier to perform external ceremonies than it is to drive away evil feelings from our hearts, that mankind in all ages have been prone to trust in them. They who think they are religious merely because they attend church regularly, and read a chapter in the Bible periodically, labor precisely under the same mistake as the Mahometan, who expects to save his soul, by travelling barefoot to Mecca, or the East Indian Fakir, who hangs with his head downward several hours each day, in order to prove his sanctity. There is no real religion that does not come from the heart; outward observances are worth nothing except they spring from inward feeling. In all ages and countries we find men willing to endure every species of privation and suffering, nay, even death itself, for the sake of going to heaven; but very few are willing that the Lord should purify their hearts from selfish feelings. Like the leper of old they are willing to do some *great* thing, but they will not obey the simple injunction to 'wash and be clean.'

This tendency to trust in what is outward is so strong in human nature that great care should be taken not to strengthen it by education. Children should always be taught to judge whether their actions are right, by the *motives* which induced the actions. Religion should be made as pleasant as possible to their feelings, and all particular rules and prohibitions should be avoided.

Quiet is the first idea which a young child can receive of the Sabbath; therefore I would take no notice of his playing with his kitten, or his blocks, so long as he kept still. If he grew noisy, I should then say to him, ' You must not make a noise to-day; for it is the Sabbath day, and I wish to be quiet, and read good books. If you run about, it disturbs me.'

I make these remarks with regard to very young children. As soon as they are old enough to read and take an interest in religious instruction, I would have playthings put away; but I would not compel them to refrain from play, before I gave them something else to interest their minds. I would make a *difference* in their playthings. The noisy rattle and the cart which have amused them during the week, should give place to picture-books, the kitten, little blocks, or any *quiet* amusement.

If the heads of a family keep the Sabbath with sobriety and stillness, the spirit of the day enters into the hearts of the children. I have seen children of three and four years old, who were habitually more quiet on Sunday than on any other day, merely from the soothing influence of example.

A child should be accustomed to attend public worship as early as possible; and the walk to and from church should be made pleasant, by calling his attention to agreeable objects. When his little heart is delighted with the lamb, or the dove, or the dog, or the flower, you have pointed out to him, take that opportunity to

7 *

tell him God made all these things, and that he has
provided everything for their comfort, because he is
very kind.   We are too apt to forget God, except in
times of affliction, and to remind children of him only
during some awful manifestation of his power; such as
thunder, lightning and whirlwind.   It certainly is proper
to direct the infant thoughts to him at such seasons; but
not at such seasons only.   A tempest produces a natural
feeling of awe, which should never be disturbed by
jesting and laughter; emotions of dependence and
reverence are salutary to mortals.   But we should speak
of God often in connexion with everything calm and
happy.   We should lead the mind to dwell upon his
infinite *goodness*; that he may indeed be regarded as a
Heavenly *Father*.

An early habit of prayer is a blessed thing.   I would
teach it to a child as soon as he could lisp the words.
At first, some simple form must be used, like, 'Now I
lay me down to sleep;' but as children grow older, it is
well to express themselves just as they feel.   A little
daughter of one of my friends, when undressed to go to
bed, knelt down of her own accord, and said, 'Our
Father, who art in heaven, forgive me for striking my
little brother to-day, and help me not to strike him
again; for oh, if he should die, how sorry I should be
that I struck him!'   Another in her evening prayer
thanked God for a little sugar dog, that had been given
her in the course of the day.   Let it not be thought for
a moment that there is any irreverence in such prayers
as these coming from little innocent hearts.   It has a
blessed influence to look to God as the source of all our
enjoyments; and as the enjoyments of a child must

necessarily be childish, it is sincere and proper for them to express gratitude in this way.

While I endeavored to make Sunday a very cheerful day, I would as far as possible give a religious character to all its conversation and employments. Very young children will become strongly interested in the Bible, if it is read to them, or they are suffered to talk about it. They will want to hear, for the hundredth time, about the little boy who said to his father, 'My head! My head!' They will tell over to each other with a great deal of delight, how he died, and was laid on his little bed, and how the prophet lay down with him, and restored him to life; and how the little boy sneezed seven times.

The story of Joseph, of Samuel, of David, of the meeting of Isaac and Rebecca at the Well, are very attractive to children. It is the first duty of a mother to make the Bible precious and delightful to her family. In order to do this, she must choose such parts as are best suited to their capacities; talk to them about it in a pleasant and familiar style; and try to get their little minds interested in what they read. If made to spell out a chapter in a cold, formal manner, and then told to go and sit down and be still, they will take no interest in the Bible; nor would they, by such means, take an interest in anything.

At no period of life should people hear the Bible spoken lightly of, or any passage quoted in jest; thoughtlessness in this respect does great mischief to ourselves and others. There cannot be a worse practice than that of making a child commit a chapter of the Scriptures as a punishment for any offence. At some schools, the Bible (being the heaviest book to be found) is held at arm's length till the little culprit gets so weary, that he would gladly throw the volume across the room.—This is very injudicious. In no way whatever should the Bible be associated with anything disagreeable.

A little hymn every Sabbath is a pleasant and profitable lesson; and if it is simple enough to be understood, the child will amuse himself by repeating it through the week. Some of the very strongest impressions of childhood are made by the hymns learned at an early age: therefore, parents should be careful what kind of ones are learned. They should first read them themselves, and *think* carefully what impressions of God, religion, and death, they are likely to convey.

As children grow older, you may add to their interest in the Scriptures by accounts of Palestine, and of the customs of the Jews. Helon's Pilgrimage to Jerusalem is a good book for this purpose. Maps, on which the travels of our Saviour and the Apostles may be traced are excellent for Sunday lessons. Such means as these give an interest to religious instruction, and prevent it from becoming a task. Perhaps some parents will be ready to say that their own education has not fitted them for thus assisting their children; but surely books and maps are cheap, and whoever has common sense, and the will to learn, cannot fail to understand them. As for the expense, it is better to give your child right feelings and enlightened ideas, than to give him dollars. You may leave him a large sum of money, but he cannot buy happiness with it, neither can he buy a good heart, or a strong mind; but if his feelings are

correct and his understanding cultivated, he will as-
suredly be happy, and will be very likely to acquire a
competency of the good things of this world.

In order to relieve the tediousness of too much reading and studying, it is a good plan for parents to walk
with children on Sabbath afternoon, for the purpose of
drawing their attention to the works of God, and
explaining how his goodness extends over all things.
The structure of a bird's nest may be made to convey
religious instruction, and inspire religious feeling, as well
as a hymn.   For this reason, books which treat of the
wonderful mechanism of the eye and the ear, the pro-
visions for the comfort of animals, and the preservation
of plants—in a word, all that leads the mind to dwell
upon the goodness and power of God,—are appropriate
books for Sunday, and may be read, or studied, to great
advantage, when children are old enough to understand
them.

But after all, religion is not so much taught by *lessons*,
as it is by our examples, and habits of speaking, acting,
and thinking.   It should not be a garment reserved only
for Sunday wear; we should always be in the habit of
referring everything to our Father in heaven.   If a
child is reminded of God at a moment of peculiar happiness, and is then told to be grateful to Him for all his
enjoyments, it will do him more good than any words
he can learn.   To see the cherry-stone he has planted
becoming a tree, and to be told that God made it grow,
will make a more lively impression on his mind, than
could be produced by any lesson from a book.   The
Friends say every day should be Sunday; and certainly
no day should pass without using some of the opportuni-

ties, which are always occurring, of leading the heart to God.

To catechisms in general I have an aversion. I think portions of the Bible itself are the best things to be learned ; and something may be found there to interest all ages. Cummings' Questions in the New Testament appear to me better than anything of the kind ; because the answers are to be found in the Bible itself ; but even in this I would blot out all answers given by the writer— I would have children learn nothing of men, but every-thing from God. It is important that Bible lessons should be accompanied with familiar and serious conver-sation with parents ; it interests a child's feelings, and enlightens his understanding. Perhaps some will think I have pointed out very arduous duties for the Sabbath, and that if so much is done for children, parents will have no time left for their own reading and reflection. But there can be no doubt that (interesting) lessons and con-versations with children are both pleasant and useful to parents ; you cannot dispose of a part of the day more satfactorily to your heart or your conscience. It is by no means necessary to devote the whole day expressly to their instruction. Let your own pursuits be such as imply a respect for the sanctity of the Sabbath, and *put them in the way* of employing themselves about what is good, as well as pleasant. Young people should always be taught to respect the employments and convenience of others ; they should learn to wait patiently for their elders to join in their studies or amusements. If you treat them with perfect gentleness, and show a willing-ness to attend to them when it is in your power, they will soon acquire the habit of waiting cheerfully. But never explain anything to a child because he is impatient and teases you, when it is really very inconvenient to you, and of no immediate consequence to him. Let your constant practice in all things show him, that you are less inclined to attend to him when he teases you, than when he waits patiently; but, at the same time, never make him wait when it is not necessary. There is no end to the wonders that may be wrought by gentleness and firmness.

The religious knowledge conveyed in early childhood should be extremely simple. It is enough to be told that God is their Father in heaven; that every thing in the world is formed by his wisdom, and preserved by his love; that he knows every thought of their hearts; that he loves them when they do what is right; and that good children, when they die, go to heaven, where God and the angels are. No opportunity should be lost of impressing upon their minds that God *loves* the creatures he has made; even for the most common enjoyments of life they should be taught to be thankful to him. When guilty of a falsehood, or any other wrong action, they should be solemnly reminded that though nobody in the world may know it, God sees it. This simple truth will make a serious impression, even when they are quite small; and as they grow older, they may be more deeply impressed, by adding that every time we indulge any evil feeling, we remove ourselves farther from God and good angels, and render ourselves unfit for heaven. It may seem like a nice metaphysical distinction, but I do think it very important that children should early, and constantly, receive the idea that the wicked *remove themselves* from God—that God never *withdraws from them.*

Divine influence is always shedding its holy beams upon the human soul, to purify and bless. It is our own fault, if our souls are in such a state that we cannot receive it.

In the whole course of education, we should never forget that we are rearing beings for another world as well as for this; they should be taught to consider this life as a preparation for a better. Human policy is apt to look no farther than the honors and emoluments of this world; but our present life is, at the longest, but an exceedingly small part of our existence; and how unwise it is to prepare for time and neglect eternity. Besides, the best way of fitting ourselves for this world is to prepare for another. Human prudence is not willing to perform every duty in earnestness and humility, and trust the rest to Providence. Yet, after all, God will do much better for us than we can do for ourselves. All our deep-laid schemes cannot make us so happy, as we should be if we were simply good. I do not mean that the active employments of life should be neglected; for I consider them as duties, which may and ought to be performed in the true spirit of religion: I mean that we should industriously cultivate and exert our abilities, as a means of usefulness, without feeling anxious about wealth or reputation. It is the doing things from a wrong motive, which produces so much disorder and unhappiness in the world.

Religious education, in early life, should be addressed to the heart, rather than to the mind. The affections should be filled with love and gratitude to God, but no attempt should be made to introduce doctrinal opinions into the understanding. Even if they could be understood, it would not be well to teach them. It is better that the mind should be left in perfect freedom to choose its creed; if the *feelings* are religious, God will enlighten the *understanding;* he who really *loves* what is good, will *perceive* what is true.

Miss Hamilton, in her excellent book on education, relates an anecdote of a mother, who tried to explain the doctrine of atonement by telling a child that God came down from heaven, and lived and died on earth, for the sins of men. The little girl looked thoughtfully in the fire for some time, and then eagerly exclaimed, ' Oh, what a good time the angels must have had, when God was gone away !'

This child, being subject to great restraint in the presence of her parents, was probably in the habit of having a frolic when they were gone; and she judged the angels by the same rule. She was not to blame for judging by what she had seen and felt. It was the only standard she could use. The error was in attempting to give her ideas altogether too vast for her infant mind. This anecdote shows how necessary it is that religious instruction should, at first, be extremely plain and simple.

There is nothing perhaps in which Christians act so inconsistently as in surrounding death with associations of grief and terror. We profess to believe that the good whom we have loved in this life, are still alive in a better and happier world; yet we clothe ourselves in black, toll the bell, shun the room where we saw them die, and weep when they are mentioned. My own prejudices against wearing mourning are very strong—nothing but the certainty of wounding the feelings of

8

some near and dear friend would ever induce me to follow the custom. However, I have no right, nor have I any wish, to interfere with the prejudices of others. I shall only speak of mourning in connexion with other things, that tend to give children melancholy ideas of death. For various reasons, we should treat the subject as cheerfully as possible. We all must die; and if we *really* believe that we shall live hereafter, under the care of the same all-merciful God, who has protected us here, why should we dread to die? Children should always hear death spoken of as a blessed change; and if the selfishness of our nature will wring some tears from us, when our friends die, they should be such tears as we shed for a brief absence, not the heart-rending sobs of utter separation. When death occurs in the family, use the opportunity to make a child familiar with it. Tell him the brother, or sister, or parent he loved is gone to God; and that the good are far happier with the holy angels, than they could have been on earth; and that if we are good, we shall in a little while go to them in heaven. Whenever he afterwards alludes to them, say they are as much alive as they were on this earth; and far happier. Do not speak of it as a thing to be regretted that they have gone early to heaven; but rather as a privilege to be desired that we shall one day go to them. This is the view which the Christian religion gives us; and it is the view we should all have, did not a guilty conscience, or an injudicious education inspire us with feelings of terror. The most pious people are sometimes entirely unable to overcome the dread of death, which they received in childhood; whereas, those whose first impressions on this subject have been pleasant, find within themselves a strong support in times of illness and affliction.

The following is extracted from Miss Hamilton's work on Education :—

'If we analyze the slavish fear of death, which constitutes no trifling portion of human misery, we shall often find it impossible to be accounted for on any other grounds than those of early association. Frequently does this slavish fear operate in the bosoms of those who know not the pangs of an accusing conscience, and whose spirits bear them witness that they have reason to have hope and confidence towards God. But in vain does reason and religion speak peace to the soul of him whose first ideas of death have been accompanied with strong impressions of terror. The association thus formed is too powerful to be broken, and the only resource to which minds under its influence generally resort, is to drive the subject from their thoughts as much as possible. To this cause we may attribute the unwillingness which many people evince towards making a settlement of their affairs; not that they entertain the superstitious notion of accelerating the hour of their death by making a will; but that the aversion to the subject of death is so strong in their minds, that they feel a repugnance to the consideration of whatever is even remotely connected with it.

'How often the same association operates in deterring from the serious contemplation of a future state, we must leave to the consciences of individuals to determine. Its tendency to enfeeble the mind, and its consequences in detracting from the happiness of life, are

obvious to common observation; but as every subject
of this nature is best elucidated by examples, I shall
beg leave to introduce two from real life, in which the
importance of early association will, I trust, be clearly
illustrated.

'The first instance I shall give of the abiding influence
of strong impressions received in infancy, is in the character of a lady who is now no more; and who was too
eminent for piety and virtue, to leave any doubt of her
being now exalted to the enjoyment of that felicity
which her enfeebled mind, during its abode on earth,
never dared to contemplate. The first view she had of
death in infancy was accompanied with peculiar circumstances of terror; and this powerful impression was, by
the injudicious language of the nursery, aggravated and
increased, till the idea of death became associated with
all the images of horror which the imagination could
conceive. Although born of a noble family, her education was strictly pious; but the piety which she witnessed was tinctured with fanaticism, and had little
in it of that divine spirit of "love which casteth out
fear." Her understanding was naturally excellent; or, in
other words, what is in our sex generally termed mas-
culine; and it was improved by the advantages of a very
superior education. But not all the advantages she
derived from nature or cultivation, not all the strength of
a sound judgment, nor all the sagacity of a penetrating
and cultivated genius, could counteract the association
which rendered the idea of death a subject of perpetual
terror to her mind. Exemplary in the performance of
every religious and every social duty, full of faith and
of good works, she never dared to dart a glance of hope

beyond the tomb. The gloomy shadows that hovered
over the regions of death made the heart recoil from
the salutary meditation; and when sickness brought the
subject to her view, her whole soul was involved in a
tumult of horror and dismay. In every illness it became the business of her family and friends to devise
methods of concealing from her the real danger. Every
face was then dressed in forced smiles, and every
tongue employed in the repetition of flattering falsehoods. To mention the death of any person in her
presence became a sort of petit treason in her family;
and from the pains that were taken to conceal every
event of this kind from her knowledge, it was easy to
conjecture how much was to be dreaded from the direful
effect such information would infallibly produce. She
might, indeed, be said

"To die a thousand deaths in fearing one."

And had often suffered much more from the apprehen-
sion, than she could have suffered from the most
agonizing torture that ever attended the hour of disso-
lution.

'Here we have an instance of a noble mind subjected
by means of early association to the most cruel bondage. Let us now take a view of the consequences of
impressing the mind with more agreeable associations
on the same subject at the same early period.

'A friend of mine, on expressing his admiration of
the cheerfulness and composure, which a lady of his
acquaintance had invariably shown on the threatened
approach of death, was thus answered: "The fortitude
you so highly applaud, I indeed acknowledge as the
first and greatest of blessings; for to it I owe the enjoy-

8 *

ment of all the mercies, which a good Providence has graciously mingled in the cup of suffering. But I take no merit to myself on its account. It is not, as you suppose, the magnanimous effort of reason; and however it may be supported by that religious principle which inspires hope, and teaches resignation, while I see those who are my superiors in every Christian grace and virtue appalled by the terrors of death, I cannot to religion alone attribute my superior fortitude. For that fortitude I am, under GOD, chiefly indebted to the judicious friend of my infancy, who made the idea of death not only familiar but pleasant to my imagination. The sudden death of an elderly lady to whom I was much attached, gave her an opportunity, before I had attained my sixth year, of impressing this subject on my mind in the most agreeable colors.

' "To this judicious management do I attribute much of that serenity, which, on the apprehended approach of death, has ever possessed my mind. Had the idea been first impressed upon my imagination with its usual gloomy accompaniments, it is probable that it would still have been there invested in robes of terror; nor would all the efforts of reason, nor all the arguments of religion, have been able in these moments effectually to tranquillize my soul. Nor is it only in the hour of real danger that I have experienced the good effects of this freedom from the slavish fear of death; it has saved me from a thousand petty alarms and foolish apprehensions, into which people of stronger minds than I can boast, are frequently betrayed by the involuntary impulse of terror. So much, my good friend, do we all owe to early education." '

To these remarks, I will add an anecdote, that came under the observation of one of my friends. A little girl saw a beloved aunt die. The child was very young, —she had no ideas at all about death,—it was her first lesson on the subject. She was much affected, and wept bitterly. Her mother led her to the bed, kissed the cheek of the corpse, and observed how smiling and happy the countenance looked. 'We must not weep for dear aunt Betsy,' said she; 'she is living now with the angels; and though she cannot come to see us, she loves us, and will rejoice when we are good. If we are good, like her, we shall go to heaven, where she is; and to go to heaven, is like going to a happy *home.*'

This conversation soothed the child's mind; she felt the cold hand, kissed the cold cheek, and felt sure that her aunt was still alive and loved her.

A year or two afterwards, this child was very ill, and they told her the doctor said she would die. She looked up smiling in her mother's face, and said, with joyful simplicity, 'I shall see dear aunt Betsy before you do, mother.' What a beautiful lesson!

So important do I consider cheerful associations with death, that I wish to see our grave-yards laid out with walks, and trees, and beautiful shrubs, as places of public promenade. We ought not to draw such a line of separation between those who are living in this world, and those who are alive in another. A cherished feeling of tenderness for the dead is a beautiful trait in the Catholic religion. The prayers that continue to be offered for the departed, the offering of flowers upon the tomb, the little fragrant wreath held in the cold hand of the dead infant, —all these things are beautiful and salutary. It may be thought such customs are merely poetic; but I think they perform a much higher use than merely pleasing the fancy; I believe they help to give permanently cheerful impressions of our last great change. It is difficult for the wisest of us to tell out of what trifles our prejudices and opinions have been gradually composed.

A friend, who had resided some time in Brazil, told an anecdote, which was extremely pleasing to me, on account of the distinct and animating faith it implied. When walking on the beach, he overtook a negro woman, carrying a large tray upon her head. Thinking she had fruit or flowers to sell, he called to her to stop. On being asked what she had in her tray, she lowered the burthen upon the sand, and gently uncovered it. It was a dead negro babe, covered with a neat white robe, with a garland around its head, and a bunch of flowers in the little hands, that lay clasped upon its bosom. 'Is this your child?' asked my friend. 'It *was* mine a few day's ago,' she said; 'but it is the Madonna's now. I am carrying it to the church to be buried. *It is a little angel now.*' 'How beautifully you have laid it out!' said the traveller. 'Ah,' replied the negro, 'that is nothing compared to the beautiful bright wings with which it is flying through heaven!'

With regard to supernatural appearances, I think they should never be spoken of as objects of terror, neither should the possibility be treated as ridiculous. If we treat such subjects with contempt and utter unbelief, we at once involve ourselves in contradiction; for we tell our children they must believe the Bible; and in the Bible they read of angels holding intercourse with men, and of the dead rising from their graves.

Some say, keep children in utter ignorance of such subjects; but that is not possible. They will find them mentioned in Scripture, and in nine tenths of the books not expressly written for childhood. Our utmost care cannot keep such ideas from entering their minds; and my own opinion is, that it is not desirable we should. I believe that children may be taught to think of supernatural appearances, not only without terror, but with actual pleasure. It is a solemn and mysterious subject, and should not be introduced uselessly; but if children asked questions of their own accord, I should answer them according to what I believed to be the truth. I should tell them I believed the dead were living, speaking and thinking beings, just like ourselves; that they were happy in heaven in proportion as they were good on earth; that in ancient times, when men were innocent, angels used to come and see them, and that they loved to see them; but that now men were so wicked they could not see angels—the holy and beautiful privilege had been lost by indulging in evil; that angels full of love watched over the good, and rejoiced when they put away a wicked thought, or conquered a wicked feeling; but that we cannot see them any more than the blind man can see the sun when it is shining upon him. I would tell them that the wicked, by indulging evil, go away from the influence of God and angels, and that is the reason they are afraid; that men who have been bad in this world are bad in another, and delight to see us indulge in sin; but that God protects us always, and we need not be afraid of anything that is evil, except the evil in our own hearts; that if we try to be good, God and his angels will guard over us and teach us what

we ought to do; and that evil spirits can have no power
to tempt us, or to make us afraid, except the power we
give them by indulging our own evil passions.

I am aware that my views on this subject will differ
from many of my readers; but through the whole of
this book I have endeavored to speak what appeared
to me to be the honest truth, without any reference
to what might be thought of it. I believe that a child
would have no sort of fear of subjects they heard thus
familiarly and plainly dealt with. In one or two instances, the experiment has been tried with perfect
success. The children to whom I allude never have
an idea of *seeing* spirits; but they think Abraham and
Jacob, who used to see them, must have been very
happy. They are familiar with the idea that if they
indulge in evil, they put themselves under the influence
of spirits like themselves; but they have not the slightest fear of *seeing* them. They know that they have
spiritual eyes, with which they see in their dreams, and
will see in heaven; and that they have bodily eyes, with
which they see the material things of this world; but
they know very well that spiritual forms cannot be seen
by the natural organs of sight.

If my advice on this mysterious subject seems to you
absurd, or impracticable, reject it, in the same freedom
that I have given it. But let me ask you one question
—Did you ever know fear upon these subjects overcome by ridicule, or by arguments to prove there were
no such things as supernatural appearances? I once
knew a strong-minded man, who prided himself upon
believing nothing which he could not see, touch, and
understand. (How he believed in the existence of his

own soul, I do not know.)   His children, from some
cause or other, had their minds excited on the subject
of visions.   The father told them it was all nonsense—
that there was not a word of truth in anything of the
sort.   'But Jesus Christ appeared to his disciples, after
he was dead,' said one of the boys.   'Oh, that was a
miracle,' replied the father : 'sit down, and I will tell
you a beautiful ghost-story.'   Then he told a long
story of a man, who several times saw his deceased
friend all dressed in white, seated in his arm-chair, wearing exactly the same wig he had always worn in his
life-time.   The story was wrought up with a good deal
of skill.   The gloom of twilight, the melancholy smile
of the phantom, the terror of the spectator, were all
eloquently described.   The children stared their eyes
almost out of their heads.   At last, the end of the story
came,—'A servant entered with a light, and the old
man in the arm-chair proved to be—a great white
dog!'
   But what was the effect on the children?   Did such
a story calm or satisfy their minds?   No.   It terrified
them greatly.   For months after, they were afraid to go
into the dark, lest they should see—a great white dog.

   While I represented the intercourse with angels as a
privilege that belonged to purity and innocence, I would
as much as possible keep from the knowledge of children all those frightful stories to which remorse and disease have given birth.   Should any such come in their
way, I would represent them as the effects of a guilty
conscience, or disordered nerves, both of which produce a species of insanity; and at the same time I

would talk of the love and protection of their heavenly
Father, reminding them that every time they resisted
what was wrong, they put themselves more and more
under the blessed influence of God and his holy angels.

CHAPTER VII.

BOOKS.

THE books chosen for young people should as far as
possible combine amusement with instruction; but it is
very important that amusement should not become a
necessary inducement. I think a real love of reading
is the greatest blessing education can bestow, particularly upon a woman. It cheers so many hours of illness and seclusion; it gives the mind something to interest itself about, instead of the concerns of one's
neighbors, and the changes of fashion; it enlarges the
heart, by giving extensive views of the world; it every
day increases the points of sympathy with an intelligent
husband; and it gives a mother materials for furnish-
ing the minds of her children. Yet I believe a real love
of reading is not common among women. I know that
the new novels are very generally read; but this springs
from the same love of pleasing excitement, which leads
people to the theatre; it does not proceed from a thirst
for information. For this reason, it has a bad effect to
encourage an early love for works of fiction; particularly such as contain romantic incidents. To be sure,
works of this kind have of late years assumed so elevated

a character, that there is very much less danger from
them than formerly. We now have true pictures of
life in all its forms, instead of the sentimental, lovesick
effusions, which turned the heads of girls, fifty years
ago. But even the best of novels should form the *recreation* rather than the *employment* of the mind; they
should only be read now and then. They are a sort of
literary confectionary; and, though they may be very
perfect and beautiful, if eaten too plentifully, they do
tend to destroy our appetite for more solid and nour-
ishing food. The same remarks apply, in a less degree,
to children's forming the habit of reading nothing but
stories, which are, in fact, *little novels*. To prevent
an exclusive and injurious taste for fiction, it is well to
encourage in them a love of History, Voyages, Travels,
Biography, &c. It may be done by hearing them read
such books, or reading with them, frequently talking
about them, and seeming pleased if they remember sufficiently well to give a good account of what they have
read. Sir William Jones, who had perhaps a greater
passion for knowledge than any other mortal, and who,
of course, became extensively useful and celebrated,
says, that when he asked questions about anything, his
mother used to say to him, 'Read your book, and you
will know.' Being an intelligent and judicious woman,
she took pains to procure such volumes as would satisfy
his inquiries; and in this way his love of books became
an intense passion; he resorted to them as the thirsty
do to a fountain. This anecdote furnishes a valuable
hint. I am aware that all cannot afford to buy books
freely; but I believe there are very few in this land of
abundance, who do not spend in the superfluities of dress

and the table, more than enough to purchase a valuable library. Besides, ample means of information are now furnished the public by social libraries, juvenile libraries, lyceums, &c. I can hardly suppose it possible that any person can really want a book, in this country, without being able to obtain it. Such being the case, it certainly is easy to follow the example of Sir William Jones's mother. For instance, a cold, stinging day in winter would naturally lead a child to say, 'I wonder how people can live near the poles; where my geography says they have six months of night and winter.' Here is a good opportunity for a parent to reply, 'I will get a book about Polar Regions, and you shall read to me, after you have learned your lessons; if I am busy, and cannot hear you, you must read by yourself, and tell me about it.'

It is by seizing hold of such incidents as these, that a real love of knowledge may be instilled. The habit of having the different members of a family take turns to read aloud, while the others are at work, is extremely beneficial. It is likewise an excellent plan for young people to give a familiar account, in writing, of what they have read, and to make their own remarks upon the subject freely; but these juvenile productions should never be shown out of the family, or praised in an exaggerated manner, likely to excite vanity; and if one child is more gifted than another, care should be taken to bestow the greatest share of encouragement on the one that needs it most. I wish the habit of reading the purest and best authors aloud was more frequent in our schools. I know not how it is, girls learn an abundance of things, but they do not acquire a *love* of reading. I know very few young ladies, among those esteemed thoroughly educated, to whom a book is really a pleasanter resource than visiting, dress, and frivolous conversation. Their *understanding* may have been well drilled in certain sciences; but knowledge has no place in their *affections*. The result is, that what they have learned at school is gradually forgotten, instead of being brought into constant use in after life. Like soldiers on parade day, they go through a certain routine, and then throw by their accoutrements as things useless for anything but *parade*. The fact is, we should always begin with the affections. What we love to do, we accomplish through all manner of obstacles; but what we do not love to do is uphill work, and will not be performed if it can be avoided. If a fondness for books be once imbibed, it is plain enough that the understanding will soon be enlightened on all interesting subjects; and a person who reads, as he drinks water when he is thirsty, is the least likely of all men to be pedantic: in all things, affectation is fond of making a greater show than reality. I once heard a woman in mixed company say, 'My dear Mrs. ——, how *can* you play whist? I cannot possibly give my attention to such trifling things; if I attempt it, my mind is immediately abstracted.' I at once set her down for a fool and a pedant. I should not have been afraid to risk a fortune that she had no *real* love of knowledge. Nature and truth have never learned to blow the trumpet, and never will. The lady whom she addressed was really intelligent and well-informed; she did not love to play whist, but she very good-naturedly consented to it, because her hostess could not otherwise make up the number requisite for the game; knowledge was the food of *her* mind, not its decoration. Miss Edgeworth has very beautifully remarked, 'We are disgusted when we see a woman's mind overwhelmed with a *torrent* of learning; that the tide of literature has passed over it, should be betrayed only by its *general fertility.*' And this will be the result, if books are loved as a resource, and a means of usefulness, not as affording opportunity for display.

I have said that reading works of fiction too much, tends to destroy a relish for anything more solid, and less exciting; but I would suggest that the worst possible thing that can be done is to prohibit them entirely, or to talk against them with undue severity. This always produces a fidgetty desire to read them; and unless the principles are very strong, they will be read by stealth. Direct prohibitions, though unquestionably necessary at times, are not likely to do great good, because they appeal to the understanding without being grounded in the heart. The best way is to allow the occasional perusal of novels, which are pure in spirit and in language. When a taste is once formed for the best novels, silly, lackadaisical ones will have no charm—they will not be read from choice. In this instance, as in others of more importance, evil is prevented from entering, by finding the mind occupied with good. Many readers, and writers too, think any book is proper for young people, which has a good moral at the end; but the fact is, some books, with a long excellent moral, have the worst possible effect on a young mind.—The morality should be *in* the book, not tacked upon the *end* of it. Vices the juvenile reader never heard of, are introduced, dressed up in alluring characters, which excite

their admiration, their love, their deepest pity; and then
they are told that these heroes and heroines were very
naughty, and that in the end they were certain to die
despised and neglected.

What is the result? The generous bosom of youth
pities the sinners, and thinks the world was a cruel
world to despise and neglect them. Charlotte Temple
has a nice good moral at the end, and I dare say was
written with the best intention, yet I believe few works
do so much harm to girls of fourteen or fifteen.

I doubt whether books which represent vice, in any
way, are suitable to be put into the hands of those,
whose principles are not formed. It is better to paint
virtue to be imitated, than vice to be shunned. Familiarity with evil is a disadvantage, even when pointed out
as an object of disgust. It is true that evil must come
in the way of the young; they will find it in books, and
they will find plenty of it in the world. It would be
useless to attempt always to keep such volumes out of
the way; but I would, as far as possible, avoid them
when a child is young, and his mind is comparatively
empty. After his principles and taste are formed, he
will view such descriptions as he ought. I do not approve of stories about naughty children; they suggest
a thousand little tricks and deceptions, which would
not otherwise be thought of. A small book by a very
excellent writer appears to me liable to this objection;
I refer to Adelaide, or Stories for Children, by a Lady
of Philadelphia.*

* In justice to one of the very best of American writers, I would remark that the book in question has no other fault than being about naughty
children. It is very natural and entertaining.

9 *

Children, especially girls, should not read anything without a mother's knowledge and sanction; this is particularly necessary between the ages of twelve and sixteen, when the feelings are all fervent and enthusiastic, and the understanding is not strengthened by experience and observation. At this period, the mind and heart are very active, and parents should take peculiar care to furnish them with plenty of innocent employment.

I had almost forgotten to mention the prejudice which some people have against all manner of fairy stories and fables, simply upon the ground that they are not strictly true. The objection does not seem to me a forcible one; because I do not believe children ever think they are true. During my own childhood, I am very sure I regarded them as just what they were,—as efforts of the imagination—dreams that had a meaning to them. I do object to reading many of these things; for they are the novels of infancy, and have a similar effect, though in a less degree. All frightful and monstrous fairy stories are indeed abominable; but I do not believe that Cinderilla, or the Glass Slipper, ever injured any child. With regard to fables, children do not believe that dogs, foxes, and birds, talk to each other; nor do they think that the writer *intended* they should believe it; therfore it cannot be injurious to their love of truth. No child, who reads those pretty little verses beginning with,

'Come up into my chamber,' said the spider to the fly,—
' 'Tis the prettiest little chamber that ever you did spy!'

believes that the spider actually talked to the fly. Children understand the moral it is intended to convey perfectly well; they know that it means we should not

allow the flattery or solicitations of others to tempt us
to what is improper and dangerous. Fables and fairy-
stories, which contain a clear and simple moral, have, I
think, a good tendency; but care should be taken to as-
certain whether the little readers understand the moral,
and to explain it clearly to them, if they do not.

Imagination was bestowed upon us by the Great
Giver of all things, and unquestionably was intended to
be cultivated in a fair proportion to the other powers of
the mind. Excess of imagination has, I know, done
incalculable mischief; but that is no argument against a
moderate cultivation of it; the *excess* of all good things
is mischievous.

A strong reason why we should indulge children in
reading some of the best fairy-stories and fables, and
young people in reading some of the best novels, is,
that we cannot possibly help their getting hold of some
books of this description; and it is never wise to forbid
what we cannot prevent: besides, how much better it
is that their choice should be guided by a parent, than
left to chance.

Of late years, the circulating libraries have been over-
run with profligate and strongly exciting works, many
of them horribly exciting. I have a deep prejudice
against the whole class. The greater the genius dis-
played, the more dangerous the effects. The necessity
of fierce excitement in reading is a sort of intellectual
intemperance; and like bodily intoxication, it produces
weakness and delirium. The Pelham novels, the
works of Byron, Maturin, Lewis, and Mrs. Radcliffe,
though very different from each other, are all liable to
this objection. They have a most unhealthy influence

upon the soul. But books that frighten and painfully excite the youthful mind, bad as they are, are not so bad as the honied poison of Thomas Moore. He does not show his cloven foot. He does not try to make us in love with sin by vindicating all its deformity; he covers it with a silver veil, and makes it float so gracefully before the young and innocent, that it seems to them a creature of light. Such books do infinitely more mischief, than those openly bad in principles and in language; for danger that is concealed is not easily avoided.

What *words* can be more delicate than Moore's 'Eveleen's Bower?' and what *thoughts* can be more indecent? Yet modest girls sing it, and think no harm.

The poems of L. E. L. cannot be charged with immodesty; but they are unreal, sentimental, and exciting. I would not put them into the hands of a young girl, particularly if she were imaginative or susceptible.

Historical works of fiction may be read in connexion with history to great advantage, at any time from fourteen years of age to twenty. There is an edition of Shakspeare, called The Family Shakspeare, in which impure sentences are entirely omitted; the historical plays in this edition would give a strong additional interest to the history of the periods they illustrate. Sir Walter Scott has furnished a novel for almost all the interesting reigns in English History. These works are not professedly religious or moral.—They are pictures of life just as it is—giving a distinct idea of the manners, costume, and superstitions, of various ages. Their influence is never in opposition to good; and to a thinking mind they afford abundant food for reflection, as well as an inexhaustible fund of amusement.

Amid the multiplicity of modern books, the old standard works are too much neglected. Young people had better read Plutarch's Lives, and Anarcharsis' Travels in Greece, than to read fifty of the best miscellaneous productions of the day. To read every new thing fosters a love of novelty and a craving for excitement; and it fritters away time and intellect to little purpose. Such books as I have recommended strengthen the mind, and fill it with something solid. They are particularly valuable on account of the classical information they contain. All women should have some classical knowledge. I do not mean that they should study Latin and Greek. I merely mean that they should have general information of the government, customs, religion, &c., of the ancients; and the reason I think it desirable is, that they cannot understand the allusions in good English books without some such knowledge.— Milton, for instance, is full of allusions to ancient customs and superstitions.

It is of very great importance that children should perfectly understand what they read. They should be encouraged to give clear and distinct accounts of what they have read; and when you are doubtful whether they know the meaning of a word, be sure to ask them. If you yourself do not know, do not hesitate to say so, and refer them to the dictionary. Some people think it diminishes respect to acknowledge ignorance; but the fear is unfounded. Good sense and good judgment command respect, whether they are accompanied by great extent of information, or not. No child ever respected a judicious parent less for saying, 'When I was young, I did not have such opportunities for learning as you have; but I know how to value knowledge; and that makes me so anxious you should learn.'

The habit, which I recommended in the third chapter of directing the attention of very little children to surrounding objects, lays an excellent foundation for obtaining clear and accurate ideas of what is read. The same habit of observation, that leads them to remark whether a thing is round or square, likewise leads them to attend to the sense of what they find in books.

I believe the multitude of little books generally put into the hands of children are an injury, rather than a benefit. Juvenile ideas are rapid and transient; and a repetition of the same thoughts makes them familiar and distinct. Ideas produce such a transient impression upon the mind of an infant, that he is never weary of hearing the same old story, over and over again; it is always new to him, because he forgets it as soon as it is repeated. The same remark is true, in different degrees, of all the various stages of childhood. It is better to read one book and understand it perfectly, than to read a dozen and understand them imperfectly. It is astonishing how much pleasure and information are lost by careless readers. An instructer once said to me, 'I heard a young lady read The Abbot, by Sir Walter Scott. When she had finished, I tried to persuade her to tell me what she thought of it, and what she remembered. "Why, after all," she replied, "Scott does not tell whether Queen Mary had sandy hair, or dark hair. I was in hopes he would, for I always wanted to know." This girl was naturally bright and intelligent; but she had not been accustomed to attend to anything, except what related to dress and personal appearance. The descriptions of Scottish scenery, the workings of religious prejudice, the intrigues of political faction, the faithful pictures of life and manners, were all lost upon her. She did not *observe* them because she had never formed the habit of observing. She read through these two volumes, so full of historical interest, without feeling interested in anything but the color of Queen Mary's hair.'

Had she never read more than half a dozen books in her life, and been called upon to give a faithful account of them, it would have been impossible for her to be so entirely unobserving of the beauties of that admirable work.

To conclude, I would suggest that it is better to have a few good books than many middling ones. It is not well for young people to have a great variety. If there are but few books in the house, and those are interesting, they will be read over and over again, and well remembered. A perpetual succession of new works induces a habit of reading hastily and carelessly; and, of course, their contents are either forgotten, or jumbled up in the memory in an indistinct and useless form.

Franklin said wisely, 'Any book that is worth reading once, is worth reading twice;' and there is much good sense in the Roman maxim, 'Read *much*, but do not read *many books*.'*

* Pliny, who gave this advice, lived long before the invention of printing; if such a precaution were necessary *then*, what would he say *now*

LIST OF GOOD BOOKS.

I HAVE prepared the following list simply with the view of assisting those who are really puzzled to choose amid the multitude of books. I do not presume to be an oracle; so far from it, I would not, if I could, make my own opinion a standard for others. But the nature of my employments has, for years past, made it my duty to read such a very large number of juvenile volumes, that I may, without vanity, hope to render some assistance to those who have seen but few. I have omitted works at all sectarian in their character, even when I thought them uncommonly excellent in other respects. I have two reasons for this. The first and strongest is, that I deem it injudicious to inculcate any peculiar religious *opinions* in early life; and the second is, that I could not conscientiously do it, without interfering with the perfect religious freedom which prevails in this land of various creeds.

I have given a pretty large list of books for quite young children, in hopes of lessening the sale of such absurd nonsense as Mother Goose, Tom Thumb, Cock Robin,—and, still worse, the unnatural horrors of Blue Beard, and Jack the Giant Killer.

My catalogue is, no doubt, very imperfect; but it is scrupulously impartial and sincere. Many excellent books may have been omitted, from ignorance, or forgetfulness; but I have mentioned none except those which I have read, and believe to be among the best of their kind.

I have not mentioned a regular series of historical books, because my design has been to confine myself

entirely to useful and entertaining *family* reading, without suggesting what may be learned at school. Believing as I do, that nothing has a greater tendency to produce real refinement, than a taste for good poetry, I could
not forbear mentioning a few unexceptionable poems in
my list; if the catalogue seem short, it must be remembered that I have selected only the purest and best.

For Children from Four to Five Years of Age.

MRS. BARBAULD'S LESSONS FOR CHILDREN. All
unite in cordially approving this lady's writings. Good
sense is clothed in very attractive simplicity, and the
thoughts are continually directed to God as the giver of
all we enjoy.

MAMMA'S LESSONS. An uncommonly excellent little
book, with well-drawn pictures.

RHYMES FOR THE NURSERY. *By the author of Original Poems.* Published by *Mahlon Day, New York.*
A remarkably fascinating book to children.

FABLES FOR THE NURSERY. Extremely entertaining
to small children, and harmless in its influence.

ORIGINAL HYMNS FOR INFANT MINDS. *By Jane
Taylor.* Miss Taylor's books are among the best in
the language. They are beautifully written; and a
spirit of mild religion pervades them all.

MY FATHER. MY MOTHER. MY BROTHER. MY
SISTER. These four are excellent little toy books,
published by *Mahlon Day, New York.*

NEW YORK CRIES, IN RHYME. Published by *do.*

LITTLE STORIES FOR LITTLE CHILDREN. *Do.*

TRAVELLERS MOUNTED ON WONDERFUL ANIMALS.
Do.

10

For Children from Five to Six Years of Age.

THE INFANT MINSTREL. A collection of pretty little stories in verse.

EASY RHYMES FOR CHILDREN. Published by *Mahlon Day*.

STORIES FOR CHILDREN IN FAMILIAR VERSE. *By Nancy Sproat*.

DITTIES FOR CHILDREN. *Do*.

A PRESENT FOR SABBATH SCHOOLS. *Do*. Mrs. Sproat's books are uncommonly good. Children are delighted with the familiar yet pure simplicity of the style. She was a Calvinist; and those strongly opposed to her creed, may here and there find a verse to which they would object.

CHILD'S BOOK OF NATURE. A series of small books, published at Lancaster, with very correct well-colored engravings of Birds and Animals.

MRS. BARBAULD'S PROSE HYMNS. In this volume religious sublimity is clothed in childlike simplicity.

MRS. TRIMMER'S INTRODUCTION TO THE KNOWLEDGE OF NATURE. Mrs. Trimmer is among the very best writers of juvenile books; her influence is pure and holy.

FRANK. *By Miss Edgeworth*. HARRY AND LUCY. *Do*. ROSAMOND. *Do*. Miss Edgeworth's books are full of practical good sense, philosophic discrimination, and pure morality. They contain nothing opposed to religion, but there is an entire absence of its life-giving spirit.

PETER PARLEY'S WINTER EVENING TALES.

PETER PARLEY'S TALES ABOUT EUROPE, ASIA, AFRICA, AND AMERICA.

PETER PARLEY'S TALES OF THE PACIFIC OCEAN.

PETER PARLEY'S TALES OF THE SEA.

PETER PARLEY'S TALES OF THE SUN, MOON, AND STARS.

RHODE ISLAND STORIES. Published by *Mahlon Day, New York.*

SAYING AND DOING, OR FRANK AND HARRY. *Do.*

SELECT POEMS FOR SMALL CHILDREN. *Do.*

GOOD EXAMPLES FOR CHILDREN. *Do.*

POETIC STORIES. *Do.*

THE LITTLE FIELD DAISY. *Do.*

For Children Seven and Eight Years of Age.

ROBERT FOWLE. An uncommonly good little book.

JAMES TALBOT. Very excellent.

HYMNS, SONGS, AND FABLES FOR CHILDREN. Published by *Carter, Hendee and Babcock.*

PLEASING STORIES. *By Mrs. Hughs.* STORIES FOR CHILDREN. *Do.* AUNT MARY'S TALES FOR GIRLS. *Do.* AUNT MARY'S TALES FOR BOYS. *Do.* Mrs. Hughs has written a great deal for children; and few have written more judiciously, or more attractively.

FRANK. *Continued. By Miss Edgeworth.* HARRY AND LUCY. *Continued. Do.*

BIOGRAPHICAL SKETCHES OF CELEBRATED MEN IN AMERICA. *From the Juvenile Miscellany.* This little volume was compiled by myself. I do not mention it on account of its having any particular merit; but because I do not know of any other volume, that contains so many biographical sketches in so cheap a form.

ADVENTURES OF CONGO, IN SEARCH OF HIS MASTER. A very great favorite with children.

BERQUIN'S CHILDREN'S FRIEND. A favorite of long standing.

THE MIRROR. *By Miss Leslie, a Lady of Philadelphia.* An uncommonly sensible and entertaining book.

THE ROBINS. *By Mrs. Trimmer.* An almost unrivalled favorite with children.

THE PARENT'S ASSISTANT. *By Miss Edgeworth.* The stories that compose these volumes,—such as Simple Susan, Forget and Forgive, Two Strings to your Bow, &c.,—may be purchased either singly or in sets.

SARAH AND HER COUSIN, OR GOODNESS BETTER THAN KNOWLEDGE.

THE NATURAL HISTORY OF INSECTS. Published by *Carter, Hendee and Babcock.*

SOPHIA MORTON.

WELL SPENT HOURS.

ROBINSON CRUSOE. *By Defoe.*

ALEXANDER SELKIRK, OR THE REAL ROBINSON CRUSOE. Published by *Mahlon Day, New York.*

THE CHILDREN'S ROBINSON CRUSOE. *By the Author of The Adventures of Congo.* I mention these three, that a choice may be taken. Defoe's work is irresistibly fascinating. It has been translated into almost all languages. Alexander Selkirk is a very small book, containing a plain, unvarnished account of just such events as happened. The Children's Robinson Crusoe (by a very religious and sensible woman) unquestionably has a purer influence than Defoe's celebrated work; more entertaining it cannot be. Defoe's hero is a wild, reckless, ignorant adventurer; the *Children's* Robinson Crusoe is well educated in mind and heart.

For Children Nine and Ten Years of Age.

METAMORPHOSES. *By Mrs. Hughs.*

ORNAMENTS DISCOVERED. *Do.*

EVENINGS AT HOME. *By Mrs. Barbauld and her brother, Doctor Aiken.* A work of first rate merit.

MORAL TALES. *By Miss Edgeworth.*

THE TWIN SISTERS. *By Miss Sandham.* The mild spirit of vital piety pervades this admirable volume.

ELLEN THE TEACHER. *By Mrs. Hofland.* An excellent book.

ALICIA AND HER AUNT. *By Do.*

THE AFFECTIONATE BROTHERS.

THE GOOD GRANDMOTHER.

LEARNING BETTER THAN HOUSE AND LANDS.

PETER PARLEY'S TALES ABOUT ANIMALS.

TALES OF TRAVELS WEST OF THE MISSISSIPPI.

COOK'S VOYAGES.

BELZONI IN EGYPT.

ADVENTURES AND DISCOVERIES IN AFRICA. *Forming part of the Family Library.* VOYAGES AND DISCOVERIES IN POLAR REGIONS. *Do.* These two volumes contain the pith and marrow of a great many interesting Voyages and Travels.

LIFE AND MAXIMS OF WM. PENN. *By Mrs. Hughs.*

For Children Eleven and Twelve Years of Age.

SANDFORD AND MERTON. Deservedly a great fafavorite, particularly with boys.

SEQUEL TO FRANK. *By Miss Edgeworth.*

SEQUEL TO HARRY AND LUCY. *Do.*

10 *

WILLIAM AND UNCLE BEN. *By Mrs. Hofland.*

THE OFFICER'S WIDOW. *Do.*

THE MERCHANT'S WIDOW. *Do.*

THE CLERGYMAN'S WIDOW. *Do.*

SON OF A GENIUS. *Do.*

THEODORE, OR THE CRUSADERS. *Do.*

POEMS AND JUVENILE SKETCHES. *By Anna Maria Wells.* Very pure thoughts in beautiful verse.

BEATITUDES. An excellent little volume.

LESSONS WITHOUT BOOKS. *By the same Author.*

SPANISH CONQUESTS. *Do.* LOUISA AND HER COUSINS. *Do.* These books are evidently written by a judicious mother, and observing woman.

THE YOUNG EMIGRANTS. *Published by Carter, Hendee and Babcock.* This is an instructive and very entertaining book. It conveys a very vivid impression of the difficulties to be surmounted in a new settlement; and the lesson it teaches is most salutary.

THE CHILDREN'S WEEK. *By the same Author.*

FRUIT AND FLOWERS. This is an excellent little book, calculated to excite gratitude and love to our heavenly Father. It favors no particular sect; though the impression it leaves is rather unfavorable to sudden and violent religious excitement.

BERTHA'S VISIT TO HER UNCLE IN ENGLAND. *In 2 vols.* This book contains a very great variety of information in a small compass. Its religious tendency is Calvinistic.

THE TRAVELLERS. *By Miss Sedgwick.*

THE COUSINS. *By Mrs. Hughs.*

EMMA MORTIMER. *By Mrs. Hughs.*

---

* Where the names of publishers are mentioned, it is to avoid confusion between two books of the same title.

A VISIT TO THE SEA-SIDE. *In 2 vols.*

TALES OF A GRANDFATHER. 1ST AND 2D SERIES. *By Walter Scott.* These volumes form a most fascinating history of Scotland.

THE LIBRARY OF ENTERTAINING KNOWLEDGE. *Published in a series of numbers.* This set is valuable in a family. Some of the numbers are unusually attractive to young people; and in all of them there is a happy combination of science and entertainment.

For Young People of Thirteen and Fourteen Years of Age.

DISPLAY, OR ELIZABETH PALMER. *By Jane Taylor.* A better book for girls of this age was never written. It is full of piety and good sense, clothed in a most pleasing form. It deserves to be printed in letters of gold.

THE COTTAGERS OF GLENBURNIE. *By Miss Hamilton.* Everybody should read this volume. It is full of practical good sense and religious benevolence.

THE NEW ENGLAND TALE. *By Miss Sedgwick.* The influence of an enlightened mind and a pure heart is shed like sunshine over all that Miss Sedgwick writes.

RASSELAS. *By Doctor Johnson.*

POPULAR TALES. *By Miss Edgeworth.*

EXILES OF SIBERIA. *By Madame Cottin.*

ILLUSTRATIONS OF LYING. *By Mrs. Opie.*

TALES OF A GRANDFATHER. 3D AND 4TH SERIES. *By Walter Scott.* Containing the history of France.

MY EARLY DAYS. *By Walter Ferguson.* A most charming little book.

NORTHWOOD. *By Mrs. Hale.*

THE SANDFORDS, OR HOME SCENES. *By Mrs. Larned.*

SKETCHES OF IRISH CHARACTER. *By Mrs. S. C. Hall.*

THE TRIALS OF MARGARET LYNDSEY.

BIOGRAPHY OF BISHOP HEBER. *Abridged for young people.*

HELON'S PILGRIMAGE TO JERUSALEM. A book useful to read in connexion with the Holy Scriptures, because it gives a very distinct idea of the customs and superstitions of the Jews.

NICHOLS' CATECHISM OF NATURAL THEOLOGY. A useful volume in connexion with Sunday lessons. Its design is to teach the power and goodness of God, by explaining the wonderful mechanism of nature.

ORIENTAL FRAGMENTS—ILLUSTRATIONS OF THE EVIDENCES OF CHRISTIANITY—and HARRY BEAUFOY. *By Maria Hack*, are likewise good books for the same purpose. The style is not sufficiently simple to attract children, but judicious parents can make great use of them, in giving religious lessons from the every-day occurrences of life.

PLUTARCH'S LIVES.

CONTRIBUTIONS OF Q. Q. *By Jane Taylor.*

For Young People from Fifteen to Sixteen Years of Age.

MRS. CHAPONE'S LETTERS.

WATTS ON THE IMPROVEMENT OF THE MIND.

TAYLOR ON SELF-CULTIVATION.

ABBOTT'S LETTERS FROM CUBA.

THE MODERN TRAVELLER. *With Maps and En-*

gravings. These volumes are published in a series intended to comprise all the best books of travels in various countries. The volumes are sold separately if desirable.

SELECTIONS FROM FENELON. *By a Lady.*

RHODA.

ISABELLA. *By the same Author.* I think these are the purest and best works of fiction that can be put into a woman's hand.

THE LADY OF THE MANOR. *By Mrs. Sherwood.* Having intended to avoid everything sectarian, I am puzzled about Mrs. Sherwood's books. She is a zealous Episcopalian, and she never writes anything that is not very strongly tinged with her own doctrines. But there is so much power and tenderness in her appeals to the heart, her characters are so true to life, and there is so much earnestness and sincerity in her religious views, that I cannot omit her name in a list of good books. The same remarks are true with regard to her numerous little books for children; they are all natural, interesting and pure—but full of Calvinism and abstract questions of theology.

THINGS BY THEIR RIGHT NAMES.

DISCIPLINE.

SELF-CONTROL.

TEMPER, OR DOMESTIC SCENES. *By Mrs. Opie.*

REDWOOD. *By Miss Sedgwick.*

HOPE LESLIE. *By Do.*

CLARENCE. *By Do.*

TALES OF FASHIONABLE LIFE. *By Miss Edgeworth.*

BELINDA. *Do.*

CASTLE RACKRENT. *Do.*

PATRONAGE. *By Miss Edgeworth.*

THE ABSENTEE. *Do.*

THE SKETCH BOOK. *By Washington Irving.*

LIFE OF COLUMBUS. *By Do.* This has been published in an abridged form, for young people.

LIFE OF LEDYARD. *By Jared Sparks.*

LIFE OF LORD COLLINGWOOD. The lessons conveyed by this book are full of all that is noble and estimable in human character.

MARSHALL'S LIFE OF WASHINGTON.

LIVES OF THE NOVELISTS. *By Walter Scott.*

LIVES OF PAINTERS AND SCULPTORS. *By Allan Cunningham. Forming a part of the Family Library.*

TRAVELS OF ANACHARSIS IN GREECE.

ROLLIN'S ANCIENT HISTORY.

GOLDSMITH'S HISTORY OF ENGLAND.

THE FAMILY SHAKSPEARE. To be read in connexion with history.

All the WAVERLEY NOVELS. Valuable as distinct pictures of human nature in all its varieties, and as charming historical records.

ROBERTSON'S HISTORY OF CHARLES FIFTH.

ROBERTSON'S HISTORY OF SCOTLAND.

ROBERTSON'S HISTORY OF AMERICA.

POETRY.

MILTON'S COMUS AND LYCIDAS. I mention these in preference to Paradise Lost, because I think very few young people can enter heartily into the sublime beauties of that magnificent poem. Comus is a most pure and beautiful model for forming the youthful taste.

COWPER'S POEMS.

WORDSWORTH'S POEMS.*
SIR WALTER SCOTT'S LADY OF THE LAKE.
MARMION.   LAY OF THE LAST MINSTREL.
THOMSON'S SEASONS.
CAMPBELL'S POEMS.
MRS. HEMAN'S POEMS.
BERNARD BARTON'S POEMS.
BRYANT'S POEMS.
MRS. SIGOURNEY'S POEMS.

CHAP. VIII.

POLITENESS.

IN politeness, as in many other things connected with
the formation of character, people in general begin outside, when they should begin inside ; instead of beginning with the heart, and trusting that to form the manners, they begin with the manners, and trust the heart
to chance influences. The *golden rule* contains the
very life and soul of politeness.   Children may be taught
to make a graceful courtesy, or a gentlemanly bow,—
but, unless they have likewise been taught to abhor
what is selfish, and always prefer another's comfort and
pleasure to their own, their politeness will be entirely
artificial, and used only when it is their interest to use

* It requires great maturity of mind, and habits of reflection, fully to appreciate Milton and Wordsworth. Scott and Campbell would probably
interest the youthful imagination more than any other poetic writers.

it. On the other hand, a truly benevolent, kind-hearted person will always be distinguished for what is called native politeness, though entirely ignorant of the conventional forms of society.

I by no means think graceful manners of small importance. They are the outward form of refinement in the mind, and good affections in the heart; and as such must be lovely. But when the form exists without the vital principle within, it is as cold and lifeless as flowers carved in marble.

Politeness, either of feeling or of manner, can never be taught by set maxims. Every-day influence, so unconsciously exerted, is all important in forming the characters of children; and in nothing more important than in their manners. If you are habitually polite, your children will become so, by the mere force of imitation, without any specific directions on the subject. Your manners at home should always be such as you wish your family to have in company. Politeness will then be natural to them; they will possess it without thinking about it. But when certain outward observances are urged in words, as important only because they make us pleasing, they assume an undue importance, and the unworthiness of the motive fosters selfishness. Besides, if our own manners are not habitually consistent with the rules we give, they will be of little avail; they will in all probability be misunderstood, and will certainly be forgotten. I, at this moment, recollect an anecdote, which plainly shows that politeness cannot be shuffled on at a moment's warning, like a garment long out of use. A worthy, but somewhat vulgar woman, residing in a secluded village, expected a visit from strangers of some distinction. On the spur of the occasion, she called her children together, and said, 'After I have dressed you up, you must sit very still, till the company comes; and then you must be sure to get up and make your bows and courtesies; and you must mind and say "Yes, ma'am," and "No, ma'am"—"Yes, sir," and "No, sir"—"I thank you."' The visitors arrived—and the children, seated together like 'four and twenty little dogs all of a row,' uprose at once, bobbed their bows and courtesies, and jabbered over, 'Yes, ma'am—no, ma'am—yes, sir—no, sir—I thank you—There, mother now we've done it!'

Foreigners charge us with a want of courtesy to each other in our usual intercourse; and I believe there is some truth in the accusation. On all great occasions, the Americans are ready, heart and hand, to assist each other; but how much more gracefully and happily the French manage in the ten thousand petty occurrences of life! And, after all, life is made up of small events. The golden chain of existence is composed of innumerable little links; and if we rudely break them, we injure its strength, as well as mar its beauty.

The happiest married couples I have ever known were those who were scrupulous in paying to each other a thousand minute attentions, generally thought too trifling to be of any importance; and yet on these very trifles depended their continued love for each other. A birth-day present, accompanied with a kind look or word—reserving for each other the most luxurious fruit, or the most comfortable chair—nay, even the habit of always saying, 'Will you have the goodness?' and 'Thank you'—all these seemingly trivial things have a great effect on domestic felicity, and on the manners of children.   Early habits of preferring others to ourselves are very important.   A child should always be taught to give away the *largest* slice of his apple, or his cake, and to take his whistle immediately from his mouth, if a sick little brother or sister is anxious for it.   I believe the easy and natural politeness of the French may in a great measure be attributed to their remarkable care in forming such early habits of self-denial.

I cordially approve of the good old fashion of never saying 'Yes,' or ' No,' to those older than ourselves.   It appears to me peculiarly proper and becoming for young persons always to rise when addressed by those whose age or character demands respect.   I am surprised to see how seldom the young give an aged person the inner side of the walk, when they meet in the street; and still more so when I see them unceremoniously push by their elders, while entering or leaving a room.

It is a graceful habit for children to say to each other, 'Will you have the goodness?'—and 'I thank you.'   I do not like to see prim, artificial children; there are few things I dislike so much as a miniature beau, or belle.   But the habit of good manners by no means implies affectation or restraint.   It is quite as easy to say, 'Please to give me a piece of pie,' as to say, 'I want a piece of pie.'

The idea that constant politeness would render social life too stiff and restrained, springs from a false estimate of politeness. True politeness is perfect ease and free-dom.   It simply consists in treating others just as you love to be treated yourself.   A person who acts from this principle will always be said to have 'sweet pretty ways with her.' It is of some consequence that your daughter should know how to enter and leave a room gracefully; but it is of prodigiously more consequence that she should be in the habit of avoiding whatever is disgusting or offensive to others, and of always preferring their pleasure to her own. If she has the last, a very little intercourse with the world will teach her the first.

I believe nothing tends to make people so awkward as too much anxiety to please others. Nature is graceful; and affectation, with all her art, can never produce any thing half so pleasing. The very perfection of elegance is to imitate nature as closely as possible; and how much better it is to have the reality than the imitation! I shall probably be reminded that the best and most unaffected people are often constrained and awkward in company to which they are unaccustomed. I answer, the reason is, they do not act themselves—they are afraid they shall not do right, and that very fear makes them do wrong. Anxiety about the opinion of others fetters the freedom of nature. At home, where they act from within themselves, they would appear a thousand times better. All would appear well, if they never tried to assume what they did not possess. Everybody is respectable and pleasing so long as he is perfectly natural. I will make no exception—Nature is *always* graceful. The most secluded and the most ignorant have some charm about them, so long as they affect nothing—so long as they speak and act from the impulses of their own honest hearts, without any anxiety as to what others think of it.

Coarseness and vulgarity are the effects of education and habit; they cannot be charged upon nature. True politeness may be cherished in the hovel as well as in the palace; and the most tattered drapery cannot conceal its winning charms.

As far as is consistent with your situation and duties, early accustom your children to an intercourse with strangers. I have seen young persons who were respectful and polite at home, seized with a most painful and unbecoming bashfulness, as soon as a guest entered. To avoid this evil, allow children to accompany you as often as possible, when you make calls and social visits. Occasional interviews with intelligent and cultivated individuals have a great influence on early character and manners, particularly if parents evidently place a high value upon acquaintances of that description. I have known the destiny of a whole family changed for the better, by the friendship of one of its members with a person of superior advantages and correct principles.

But it must be remembered that a call, or a social visit, may be made almost as injurious as a party, if children are encouraged in showing off, or constantly habituated to hearing themselves talked about. Much as the failing has been observed and laughed at, it is still too common for mothers to talk a great deal about their children. The weariness with which strangers listen to such domestic accounts is a slight evil compared with the mischief done to children, by inducing them to think themselves of so much importance: they should never be taught to consider themselves of any consequence, except at home in the bosom of their own families.

Nothing tends to foster the genuine politeness which springs from good feeling, so much as scrupulous attention to the aged. There is something extremely delightful and salutary in the free and happy intercourse of the old and young. The freshness and enthusiasm of youth cheers the dreariness of age; and age can return the benefit a hundred fold, by its mild maxims of experience and wisdom. In this country, youth and age are too much separated; the young flock together, and leave the old to themselves. We seem to act upon the principle that there cannot be sympathy between these two extremes of life; whereas there may be, in fact, a most charming sympathy—a sympathy more productive of mutual benefit than any other in the world.

The aged, from the loneliness of their situation, the want of active employment, and an enfeebled state of health, are apt to look upon the world with a gloomy eye; and sometimes their gloom is not unmixed with bitterness : hence arises the complaint of their harshness and asperity towards the follies of youth. These evils, so naturally growing out of their isolated situation, would seldom gain power over the old, if they were accustomed to gentleness, attention, and deference from the young; they would be softened by juvenile love, and cheered by juvenile gaiety. Such intercourse sheds a quiet brightness on the decline of life, like sunshine on a weather-beaten tree, or a moss-covered dwelling. What is there on earth more beautiful than an aged person full of content and benevolence !

In China, it is the custom for young people always to stand with head uncovered in the presence of their seniors. Perhaps this is carrying the outward forms of respect to an inconvenient excess; but the *principle* is true to nature and goodness. The mere circumstance of

11 *

being old should insure peculiar deference and attention even from strangers. It is considered a sign of a good heart to love little children; I think spontaneous kindness for the aged is a much better proof. I have seen gentlemen, who, in mixed companies, always bestowed the largest share of attention upon the old and neglected.—Had I a beloved daughter, I would choose such a man for her husband.

The German custom of giving Christmas presents to parents, brothers, and sisters, has a happy influence upon the affections, and of course upon the manners. The enjoyment is entirely anti-selfish—it consists in the experience, that 'it is more blessed to *give* than to *receive*.' What can be purer than the eager pleasure of a group of children busy in preparing a gift for a parent, and anxious to keep their little secret, in order to produce a joyful surprise? If their offerings are of their own manufacture, a double good is produced; both ingenuity and love are excited, and the motive that excites them is holy. It has a good effect for parents to place a superior value upon whatever children make themselves—such as all the varieties of needle-books, pin-cushions, boxes, &c.

One very prevalent fault among children is a want of politeness to domestics. Young people should not, from mere whim and caprice, be allowed to make demands upon the time and patience of those who are hired to attend upon the family. They should make no unnecessary trouble in the kitchen; and when they ask for anything, they should speak politely—saying, 'Will you have the goodness?' 'I thank you,' &c. Such conduct greatly tends to make domestics more respectful, kind, and obliging. Miss Edgeworth, in her work on Education, recommends that children should never be allowed to speak a single word to a servant; and that they should be kept in a part of the house entirely remote, for fear of contamination. Such a system cannot be carried into effect in this country; and I am thankful it cannot. A child cannot know the nature of such an injunction,—his inexperienced mind cannot form an idea of the frightful and vulgar stories his mother dreads his hearing in the kitchen. He is told not to talk with the domestics, and he at once conceives an idea of superiority, and thinks he is not bound to pay any regard to their feelings or happiness. This principle is a bad one, under any form of government; but in our country its application is peculiarly preposterous; for those who are servants now may be mistresses next year; and those who *keep* domestics now may *be* domestics hereafter. Still, I think it is very injurious to children to form a habit of staying in the kitchen; not on account of any difference in station,—but because we change domestics so frequently in this country, and must necessarily be often uncertain as to their habits and principles. If I were sure that a girl was conscientious, and never told vulgar or superstitious stories, I should be perfectly willing to trust children of any age to her influence. And even if she were a stranger to me, I would never *forbid* a child's going into the kitchen, or *advise* him not to talk with her. I should rather he would run the risk of hearing a vulgar, or superstitious story, than to infest his spirit with pride. But though I would never give children any rules to this effect, I would by a *silent influence* keep them

with myself as much as possible. I would make the
parlor pleasant to them—I would supply them with
interesting employment—I would do everything to
promote full confidence and companionship between
them and their parents—I would make the bond
between brothers and sisters strong, by fostering mutual
love, by teaching them to speak politely, to act kindly,
to regard each other's wants, and respect each other's
property. By these means, the mind and the heart
would be so occupied, that children would have no
temptation to spend their evenings in the kitchen. But
my motive for pursuing such a guarded course, would
be no idea of superiority (for I acknowledge none, but
degrees of goodness); I would withdraw them from the
influence of domestics merely because there is a chance
that such influence will be impure. If I were certain
of the good principles and judicious conversation of a
girl, I should not deem precaution necessary. And one
thing is certain,—a domestic who is worthy of being
kept in your house, is worthy of being treated with
kindness and perfect politeness; and children should
be early instructed never to speak rudely, or make
unnecessary demands upon her time and patience. I
am aware that there are peculiar difficulties attending
this relation in our republican country,—there is mutu-
ally too much jealousy of being encroached upon. But
it is one of the evils which grow out of a multitude of
blessings; and whether a domestic be ungrateful or not,
it will be a satisfaction that you have done your duty,
and taught your children to do theirs.

In connexion with politeness, I would again allude to
the great importance of *habits of observation*. What

is called native politeness is entirely the result of kind feelings combined with habits of attention. Everybody has observed that men of the world have a wonderful facility in adapting themselves to all varieties of character. Their faculty of pleasing everybody seems like instinct, yet, in fact, it is merely the result of close observation. People who have bad hearts can attain this power, and exert it when they choose, from no other excitement but vanity, or self-interest. But this is no reason why the same power should not be exerted to good purposes, and with good motives.

A ready discrimination of character is attained by habits of observation; and merely from a want of these habits, excellent hearted people often make blunders painful to themselves and others. We all know by our own feelings, that it is not pleasant to have the attention of strangers called to any personal defect we may have; yet well meaning people will sometimes strangely persist in such conversation.—They will not only ask what produced a scar, but they will insist upon knowing how long you have been troubled with it, whether the distemper is hereditary in your family, and whether you ever expect it will appear again. It is a chance if they do not gratuitously add stories of half a dozen individuals, who died of the same disorder, or bestowed it upon their children.

Some people are singularly perverse in praising such qualities as their hearers do not possess, and perhaps have no means of possessing. For instance, talking to the poor about the great power and influence of wealth, —enlarging upon the prodigious advantages of intelligence and learning to the uneducated—and flying into raptures about beauty in presence of the ugly and deformed. Now, in all these instances, a little *attention* to the movements of our own minds would teach us at once how to apply the golden rule.

In our intercourse with others, it should be our object to discover what they wish to *hear*, not what we wish to *say*. Literary people are often unpleasant companions in mixed society, because they frequently have not the power of adapting themselves to others. They have given their attention to books more than to characters; and they talk on such subjects as please themselves, without thinking whether they will please others. What is called affectation and pedantry, is half the time mere heedlessness and want of observation.

Mrs. Madison was esteemed the most thoroughly polite woman in America. Others might perhaps enter a room as gracefully, or superintend at table with as much dignity; the secret of her power lay in her wonderful adaptation to all sorts of characters. She was emphatically an *observing woman*. As Jefferson had no wife, she presided sixteen years at Washington;* during all which time, she is said never to have forgotten the most trifling peculiarities of character, that had once come under her observation: she always remembered them, and fashioned her conversation accordingly. Some may object to the exercise of this power, lest it should lead to insincerity; and the charge may well be brought against that kind of false politeness, which springs merely from a love of popularity. Politeness is not the only good

* When the president has no wife, or daughter, at Washington, the lady of the highest officer in the cabinet presides at the mansion on all state occasions.

thing corrupted by an unworthy motive; all precious coins have a counterfeit. When we are polite to others entirely for *our own sakes,* we are deceitful; nothing selfish has truth and goodness in it. But there is such a thing as true politeness, always kind, but never deceitful. It is right to cherish good-will toward all our fellow-creatures, and to endeavor to make them as happy as we conscientiously can. The outward forms of politeness are but the expressions of such feelings as should be in every human heart. It would be wrong to tell people we love them dearly, when in fact we know nothing about them; or to urge them to visit our houses, when we do not want to see them. But we are bound to be kind and attentive to all our fellow-creatures, when they come in our way, and to avoid giving them any unnecessary pain, by our manners or conversation.

In order to teach children the right sort of politeness, it must be taught through the agency of a pure motive. They should not be taught to observe and respect the feelings of others for the sake of making themselves pleasing, but merely because it is kind and benevolent to do so.

If I saw a child point out the patched or ragged garment of a poor companion, I would not say, 'You must not laugh at her clothes; if you do, she will think you are proud'—I would say, 'It grieves me very much to see you so unkind. If your mother were poor, and could not afford to get you new clothes, would it not hurt your feelings to be laughed at? Does not the Bible tell you to do to others as you would wish to have them do to you?   You must observe this precious rule in little things, as well as in great things.'

From the foregoing hints, it will be seen that true politeness is the spontaneous movement of a good heart and an observing mind.   Benevolence will teach us tenderness towards the feelings of others, and habits of observation will enable us to judge promptly and easily what those feelings are.

Outward politeness can be learned in set forms at school ; but at the best, it will be hollow and deceptive. Genuine politeness, like everything else that is genuine, must come from the heart.

CHAP. IX.

BEAUTY.—DRESS.—GENTILITY.

Wherever there is hypocrisy, or an apparent necessity for hypocrisy, there is something wrong.   In the management of children, are we sincere on the subject of beauty ?   When we see a handsome person, or a handsome animal, they hear us eagerly exclaim, 'Oh, how beautiful !'   'What a lovely creature !'   'What pretty eyes !'   'What a sweet mouth !' &c.   Yet when children say anything about beauty, we tell them it is of no value at all—that they must not think anything about beauty—'handsome is that handsome does,' &c.

The influence would be very contradictory, did not the eagerness of our exclamations and the coldness of our

moral lessons both tend to the same result; they both give
children an idea that the subject is of great importance.
'Mother *tells* me beauty is of no consequence, because
she thinks I shall be vain; but I am sure she and everybody else seem to *think* it is of consequence,' said a
shrewd little girl of ten years old.

It certainly is natural to admire beauty, whether it
be in human beings, animals, or flowers; it is a principle implanted within the human mind, and we cannot
get rid of it. Beauty is the outward form of goodness;
and that is the reason we love it instinctively, without
thinking why we love it. The truth is, beauty is really
of *some* consequence; but of very small consequence
compared with good principles, good feelings, and
good understanding. In this manner children ought to
hear it spoken of. There should be no *affected* indifference on this or any other subject. If a child should
say, 'Everybody loves Jane Snow—she is so pretty,'
I would answer, 'Is Jane Snow a good, kind little girl?
I should be pleased with her pretty face, and should
want to kiss her, when I first saw her; but if I found
she was cross and selfish, I should not love her; and I
should not wish to have her about me.' In this way
the attention will be drawn from the subject of beauty,
to the importance of goodness; and there is no affectation in the business—the plain truth is told. We do
love beauty at first sight; and we do cease to love it, if
it be not accompanied by amiable qualities.

Beauty is so much more obvious than the qualities of
the mind and heart, and meets so much more of spontaneous admiration, that we should be very much on
our guard against increasing the value of a gift, which

is almost unavoidably over-rated. But we must remember that our common and involuntary modes of speaking are what form the opinions of a child; moral maxims have little, or no effect, if they are in opposition to our usual manner of speaking and acting. For this reason, I would never call attention to beauty; and if dwelt upon with delighted eagerness by others, I would always remark, ' She looks as if she had a sweet *disposition*, or a bright *mind*,'—thus leading the attention from mere outward loveliness to moral and intellectual beauty. I would even avoid constantly urging a child to put on a bonnet, lest she should be tanned. I should prefer the simple reason, ' It is proper to wear a bonnet out of doors; don't you know mother always wears one, when she goes out?' I would rather a girl should have her face tanned and freckled by heat, than have her mind tanned and freckled by vanity.

Perhaps there is no gift with which mortals are endowed, that brings so much danger as beauty, in proportion to the usefulness and happiness it produces. It is so rare for a belle to be happy, or even contented, after the season of youth is past, that it is considered almost a miracle. If your daughter is handsome, it is peculiarly necessary that she should not be taught to attach an undue importance to the dangerous gift; and if she is plain, it certainly is not for her happiness to consider it as a misfortune.

For the reasons above given, I would restrain myself in expressing admiration of beauty; and when others expressed it, I would always ask, ' Is she good?' Is she amiable?' &c. I would even act upon this system toward a very little child. 1 would not praise the beauty of his kitten; and if he himself said, 'Oh, what a pretty puss! How I love her!' I would answer, 'She is a pretty puss, and a good puss. If she were cross, and scratched me every time I touched her, I should not love her, though her fur is so pretty.' All this caution is perfectly consistent with truth. I would never say that beauty was of no consequence in my opinion; because I could not say it truly.

With regard to dress, as in most other cases, a medium between two extremes is desirable. A love of finery and display is a much more common fault than neglect of personal appearance; both should be avoided. Some parents teach their children to judge everybody's merit by their dress; they do not of course say it, in so many direct words—but their influence produces that effect. What else can be the result of hearing such expressions as the following?—'Mr. —— is very much of a gentleman; he is always remarkably well dressed.' 'Is such a lady a desirable acquaintance? I presume she is; for she is always very genteelly dressed.'

There are some people, who go to the opposite extreme, and represent any attention to dress as unworthy of a strong mind; becoming costume is in their eyes a mark of frivolity. I hardly know which of the two extremes is the worse. Extravagance in dress does great mischief both to fortune and character; but want of neatness, and want of taste are peculiarly disgusting. If finery betrays a frivolous mind, sluttishness and bad taste certainly betray an ill-regulated one. Neatness and taste naturally proceed from a love of order. A mother should not talk about dress, for the same reasons that she should not talk about beauty; but she should be careful to have her own dress always neat, and well-fitted, and to show a pure and delicate taste in the choice of colors. By these means, children will form the habit of dressing well, without ever thinking much about it; the habit will be so early formed, that it will seem like a gift of nature. Miss Hamilton gives, in one short sentence, all that can be said upon the subject ; she says, 'Always dress in good taste ; but let your children see that it employs very little of your time, less of your thoughts, and none at all of your affections.'

The wish to place children in as good society as possible is natural and proper ; but it must be remembered that *genteel* society is not always *good* society. If your manners and conversation imply more respect for wealth than for merit, your children, of course, will choose their acquaintance and friends according to the style they can support, not according to character.   Let your family see that you most desire the acquaintance of those who have correct principles, good manners, and the power of imparting information.   I have heard mothers say, ' To be sure Mr. and Mrs. —— do not bear a very good character; but they live in a great deal of style ; they give beautiful parties ; and it is very convenient to have the friendship of such people.' What sort of morality can be expected of a family who have been accustomed to such maxims?   What heartless, selfish, unprincipled beings are formed by such lessons ! If they do not succeed in attaining the splendor they have been taught to covet, they will be envious, jealous, and miserable ; if they do attain it, the most that can be said is, they will spend their thousands in trying to *appear* happy before the world.

Human ambition and human policy labor after happiness in vain; goodness is the only foundation to build upon. The wisdom of past ages declares this truth, and our own observation confirms it; all the world acknowledge it; yet how few, how very few, are willing to act upon it! We *say* we believe goodness is always happiness, in every situation of life, and that happiness should be our chief study; we know that wealth and distinction do not bring happiness; but we are anxious our children should possess them, because they *appear* to confer enjoyment. What a motive for immortal beings!

If the inordinate love of wealth and parade be not checked among us, it will be the ruin of our country, as it has been, and will be, the ruin of thousands of individuals. What restlessness, what discontent, what bitterness, what knavery and crime, have been produced by this eager passion for money! Mothers! as you love your children, and wish for their happiness, be careful how you cherish this unquiet spirit, by speaking and acting as if you thought wealth the greatest good. Teach them to consider money valuable only for its use; and that it confers respectability only when it is used well. Teach them to regard their childish property as things held in trust for the benefit and pleasure of their companions—that the only purpose of having anything to call their own is that they may use it for the good of others. If this spirit were more inculcated, we should not hear children so often say, ' Let that alone; it is mine, and you sha'n't have it.' Neither should we see such an unprincipled scrambling

12 *

for wealth—such willingness to cast off the nearest
and dearest relations in the pursuit of fashion—such
neglect of unfortunate merit—and such servile adula-
tion to successful villany. I will not mention religion,
—for its maxims have nothing in common with worldly
and selfish policy,—I will simply ask what *republican-
ism* there is in such rules of conduct?

But there are always two sides to a question. If it
is pernicious to make money and style the standard of
respectability, it is likewise injurious and wrong to foster
a prejudice against the wealthy and fashionable. If we
experience the slightest degree of pleasure in discover-
ing faults or follies in those above us, there certainly is
something wrong in our own hearts. Never say to your
family, ' Such a one feels above us '—' Such a one is too
proud to come and see us '—&c. In the first place,
perhaps it is not true; (for I know by experience that
the poor are apt to be unreasonably suspicious of the
rich; they begin by being cold and proud to their
wealthy acquaintance, for fear the wealthy mean to be
cold and proud to them;) and even if it be true that a
rich neighbor is haughty, or even insolent, you should
be careful not to indulge bad passions, because he does.
Your business is with your own heart—keep that pure
—and measure out to the rich man, as well as the poor
man, just as much of respect and regard as their characters deserve, and no more.

Do not suffer your mind to brood over the external
distinctions of society. Neither seek nor avoid those
who are superior in fortune; meet them on the same
ground as you do the rest of your fellow-creatures.

There is a dignified medium between cringing for notice, and acting like a cat that puts up her back and spits, when no dog is coming.

Perhaps I say more on this subject than is necessary or useful. I am induced to say it, from having closely observed the effect produced on society by the broad and open field of competition in this country. All blessings are accompanied with disadvantages; and it is the business of the judicious to take the good and leave the evil. In this country, every man can make his own station. This is indeed a blessing. But what are some of the attendant dangers? Look at that parent, who is willing to sacrifice her comfort, her principles, nay, even her pride, for the sake of pushing her children into a little higher rank of life.

Look at another, too independent for such a course. —Hear how he loves to rail about the aristocracy— how much pleasure he takes in *showing* contempt of the rich. Is his own heart right? I fear not. I fear that unbending independence, so honorable in itself, is mixed with a baser feeling. The right path is between extremes. I would never creep under a door, neither would I refuse to enter when it was opened wide for my reception.

Poverty and wealth have different temptations, but they are equally strong. The rich are tempted to pride and insolence; the poor to jealousy and envy. The envious and discontented poor invariably become haughty and overbearing when rich; for selfishness is equally at the bottom of these opposite evils. Indeed, it is at the bottom of all manner of evils.

CHAP. X.

MANAGEMENT DURING THE TEENS.

The period from twelve to sixteen years of age is extremely critical in the formation of character, particularly with regard to daughters. The imagination is then all alive, and the affections are in full vigor, while the judgment is unstrengthened by observation, and enthusiasm has never learned moderation of experience. During this important period, a mother cannot be too watchful. As much as possible, she should keep a daughter *under her own eye ;* and, above all things, she should encourage *entire confidence towards herself.* This can be done by a ready sympathy with youthful feelings, and by avoiding all unnecessary restraint and harshness. I believe it is extremely natural to choose a mother in preference to all other friends and confidants; but if a daughter, by harshness, indifference, or an unwillingness to make allowance for youthful feeling, is driven from the holy resting place, which nature has provided for her security, the greatest danger is to be apprehended. Nevertheless, I would not have mothers too indulgent, for fear of weaning the affections of children. This is not the way to gain the perfect love of young people; a judicious parent is always better beloved, and more respected, than a foolishly indulgent one. The real secret is, for a mother never to sanction the slightest error, or imprudence, but at the same time to keep her heart warm and fresh, ready to sympathize with all the innocent gaiety and enthusiasm of youth. *Salutary* restraint, but not *unnecessary* restraint, is desirable.

I will now proceed to state what appears to me peculiarly important at the age I have mentioned; and I trust the hints I may suggest will prove acceptable to judicious parents. Heedlessness is so commonly the fault of the teens, that I shall first mention the great importance of habits of order, and neatness. The drawers, trunks and work-box of a young lady should be occasionally inspected, for the purpose of correcting any tendency to wastefulness, or sluttishness. Particular care should be taken of the teeth; they should be washed with a clean brush and water at least twice a day; to cleanse them just before retiring to rest promotes sweetness of breath, and tends to preserve them from decay. Buttons off, muslins wrinkled, the petticoat below the edge of the gown, shoestrings broken, and hair loose and straggling, should never pass unnoticed. Serious advice from a father on these subjects does more good than anything else. Smooth, well arranged hair, and feet perfectly neat, give a genteel, tasteful appearance to the whole person.

A dress distinguished for simplicity and freshness is abundantly more lady-like than the ill-placed furbelows of fashion. It is very common to see vulgar, empty-minded people perpetually changing their dresses, without ever acquiring the air of a gentlewoman. If there is simplicity in the choice of colors,—if clothes fit well, and are properly pinned, tied and arranged,—if they always have a neat, fresh look,—and above all, if the head and the feet are always in order,—

nothing more is required for a perfectly lady-like appearance.

Nothing tends to produce a love of order so much as the very early habits of observation, and attention to trifles, which I have so particularly urged in various parts of this book. I would teach a daughter to observe such trifling things as the best manner of opening a new piece of tape; and I would take every precaution to conquer the spirit that leads young people to say 'I don't care,' 'No matter how it is done,'—&c.

I have, in a previous chapter, spoken of the effect which habits of observation have upon politeness of manner; and I cannot, while speaking of an age peculiarly liable to affectation, pass by the subject of good manners without saying a few words more concerning that most disgusting and injurious fault. Let all your influence be exerted to check the slightest appearance of affectation. No matter whether it be affectation of goodness, of learning, of sentimentality, of enthusiasm, of simplicity, or of gracefulness.—It will start up in a multitude of new forms, like the fabled heads of the hydra—but cut them off unsparingly. This fault, with its most artful covering, is easily detected; nature has a quiet sincerity about her, that cannot be mistaken, or counterfeited. An absence of all *anxiety* to appear well, is the very surest way to be attractive. An entire forgetfulness of self, and a good-natured wish to oblige and amuse others, produce a feeling of ease in company, and more effectually give the stamp of refined society, than all the affectation and finery in the world. Bashfulness is very unbecoming and awkward, while modesty is peculiarly fascinating to every one. People are bashful when they are thinking about themselves and are *anxious* to appear well; they are modest when they forget themselves, and are simply *willing* to do what they can to make others happy. Proud people, unless they have long been accustomed to taking the lead in society, are very apt to be bashful; modesty and humility generally go together. Selfishness is the cause of bashfulness, as well as of more serious evils.

Habits of order should be carried into expenses. From the time children are twelve years old, they should keep a regular account of what they receive, and what they expend. This will produce habits of care, and make them think whether they employ their money usefully. It is an excellent plan for a father, at the beginning of the year, to state what he is willing each child, older than twelve, should expend per quarter. At first, the greater part might be under a mother's direction, for clothes, and other necessaries; and only a small portion be at the disposal of the child. In this way, a father knows certainly what he expends for each; and domestic discord is not likely to be produced by bills unexpectedly large. When the arrangement is once made, nothing should be added; the idea of being helped out of difficulties brought on by thoughtlessness and extravagance, would defeat the express purpose of an allowance. A mother can generally tell very nearly what it is necessary and proper for a daughter to expend yearly; if you find you really have not allowed enough, make larger provision the next year; but never add to what was originally agreed upon, except under very extraordinary circum-

stances. At sixteen years of age, or perhaps sooner,
where there is great maturity of character, a young
lady may be profited by being trusted with the whole
of her allowance, to spend at discretion; always, however, rendering an exact account to her parents, at the
end of the year.

Some may think such a system could be pursued only
by the wealthy; but it is no matter whether the quar-
terly allowance is fifty dollars, or fifty cents—the principle is the same. The responsibility implied by such
trust gives children more self-respect, and self-command;
it helps them to remember how much they owe to the
generosity of parents; and checks their heedlessness in
the expenditure of money. But its most important use
is in teaching them to be really benevolent. Children
who go to a parent and ask for things to give away,
may know what kind *impulses* are, but they know
nothing about real benevolence of *principle*. True
generosity is a willingness to deny ourselves for the
benefit of others—to give up something of our own, that
we really like, for the sake of doing good. If a child
has a quarter of a dollar a month to expend, and gives
half of it to a poor sick neighbor, instead of laying it
up to buy a book, or a trinket, he knows more of real
benevolence, than could be taught by all the books
and maxims in the world. When you know of any
such action, let a child see that it increases your affection and respect. Do not let the hurry of business, or
the pressure of many cares, keep you from expressing
marked approbation. Human nature is weak, and
temptation strong. Young people need to be cheered
onward in the path of goodness; and they should never

be disappointed in the innocent expectation of giving pleasure to a parent. But do not praise them in the presence of others; and do not say much about it, as if it were any great thing—merely treat them with unusual affection and confidence. Do not compensate their benevolence by making them presents. This will lead them into temptation. It will no longer be self-denial in them to give; for they will be sure they shall lose nothing in the end. They should learn to take pleasure in losing their own gratifications for the benefit of others.

One very good effect resulting from keeping an exact account of expenses, had well nigh escaped my memory. Should your daughter ever become a wife, this habit will enable her to conform more easily to her husband's income. A great deal of domestic bitterness has been produced by a wife's not knowing, or not thinking, how much she expends. Every prudent man wishes to form some calculation about the expenses of his family; and this he cannot do, if a wife keeps no accounts, or keeps them irregularly.

In connexion with this subject, I would urge the vast importance of a thorough knowledge of arithmetic among women. It is a study that greatly tends to strengthen the mind, and produce careful habits of thought; and no estate can be settled without it. In England and France, it is no uncommon thing for the wife of a great manufacturer or merchant to be his head clerk.

An American lady, now residing in Paris, is said to be an invaluable partner to her wealthy husband, on account of her perfect knowledge of his extensive busi-

ness, and the exact and judicious manner in which she
conducts affairs during his absence. I do not wish to
see American women taking business out of the hands
of men; but I wish they were all *capable* of doing business, or settling an estate, when it is *necessary*. For
this purpose, a very thorough knowledge of book-keeping should be attained; both the old and the new system should be learned. Nor should a general knowledge
of the *laws* connected with the settlement of estates be
neglected. Every young person ought to be well acquainted with the contents of Sullivan's Political Class-
Book. Many a widow and orphan has been cheated in
consequence of ignorance on these subjects.

Should your daughter never have an estate to settle,
or business to transact, her knowledge of arithmetic,
book-keeping and penmanship may be valuable to her
as a means of support. I do think children should be
brought up with a dread of being dependent on the
bounty of others. Some young ladies think it a degradation to support themselves; and to avoid it, they are
willing to stay with any relation, who will furnish them
a home. This is not indulging a right spirit. We ought
to be resigned and cheerful in a dependent situation,
when we cannot possibly provide for ourselves; but a
willingness to burthen others, when we can help it by
a little exertion, is not resignation—it is mere pride
and indolence. Next to a love of usefulness, knowledge
should be valued because it multiplies our resources in
case of poverty. This unwillingness to subsist on the
bounty of others should not be taught as a matter of pride,
but of principle; it should proceed from an unwillingness
to take away the earnings of others, without rendering

some equivalent, and a reluctance to share what properly belongs to the more unfortunate and needy. There is nothing selfish in this. It springs from a real regard to the good of others.

I would make it an object so to educate children that they could, in case of necessity, support themselves respectably. For this reason, if a child discovered a decided talent for any accomplishment, I would cultivate it, if my income would possibly allow it. Everything we add to our knowledge, adds to our means of usefulness. If a girl have a decided taste for drawing, for example, and it be encouraged, it is a pleasant resource, which will make her home agreeable, and lessen the desire for company and amusements; if she marry, it will enable her to teach her children without the expense of a master; if she live unmarried, she may gain a livelihood by teaching the art she at first learned as a mere gratification of taste. The same thing may be said of music and a variety of other things, not generally deemed *necessary* in education. In all cases it is best that what is learned should be learned well. In order to do this, good masters should be preferred to cheap ones. Bad habits, once learned, are not easily corrected. It is far better that children should learn one thing thoroughly, than many things superficially. Make up your mind how much you can afford to spend for one particular thing; and when you have decided that, spend it as far as it will go in procuring really good teachers. I believe this to be the best economy in the end. It is better to take twelve lessons from a first rate French teacher, than to take a hundred from one who does not know how to speak the language; be-

cause in the latter case, bad habits of pronunciation will
be learned, and probably never corrected.   The same
thing is true of all kinds of knowledge, solid or ornamental.

While speaking of acquirements, I would again urge
the great necessity of *persevering* in whatever pursuits
are commenced.   Time, talent, and money, are often
shamefully wasted by learning a variety of things imperfectly, because they prove more difficult than was at first
imagined; and what is worst of all, every individual instance of this kind, strengthens the pernicious habit of
being easily discouraged at obstacles.   A young lady
should be very sure she knows her own mind before she
begins any pursuit; but when it is once begun, it should
be an unalterable law that she *must* persevere.

Perhaps some parents of moderate fortune will ask if
there is no danger of unfitting girls for the duties of their
station, and making them discontented with their situation in life, by teaching them accomplishments merely
ornamental.   For myself, I do not believe that *any* kind
of knowledge ever unfitted a person for the discharge
of duty, *provided that knowledge was acquired from a
right motive.*   It is wonderful what different results the
same thing will produce, when the motives are different.
No matter what is learned, provided it be acquired as a
means of pleasing a parent, of becoming useful to
others, or of acquiring a necessary support.   If you
induce children to learn any particular thing for the
sake of showing off, or being as grand as their neighbors, then, indeed, you *will* unfit them for their duties,
and make them discontented with their situation.   Looking to others for our standard of happiness is the sure

way to be miserable. Our business is with our own hearts, and our own motives. When I say that a decided talent for any pursuit should be encouraged, I do not mean that every whim and caprice should be indulged. Mothers often talk about giving their daughters a *taste* for music, and a *taste* for painting, when in fact they only wish to excite in them a silly ambition to have as many accomplishments to show off, as other girls have. The consequence is, such families undertake to do a multitude of things, and do nothing well. A good deal of money is spent to very little purpose; for such young ladies do not really take *pleasure* in their employments; and if left destitute, they could not *teach* what they do not half understand.

My idea is this—First, be sure that children are familiar with all the duties of their present situation; at the same time, by schools, by reading, by conversation, give them as much *solid* knowledge as you can,—no matter how much, or of what kind,—it will come in use some time or other; and lastly, if your circumstances are easy, and you can afford to indulge your children in any matter of taste, do it fearlessly, without any idea that it will unfit them for more important duties. Neither learning nor accomplishments do any harm to man or woman if the *motive* for acquiring them be a proper one; on the contrary, those who know most, are apt to perform their duties best—provided the heart and the conscience have been educated as well as the understanding. I believe a variety of knowledge (acquired from such views as I have stated) would make a man a better servant, as well as a better president; and make a woman a better wife, as well

13 *

as a better teacher. A selfish use of riches leads to avarice, pride, and contempt of manual exertion; a selfish use of knowledge leads to pedantry, affectation, unwillingness to conform to others, and indolence in any pursuit not particularly pleasing to ourselves. But the fault is not in the riches, or the knowledge—the difficulty lies in the *selfish use* of these advantages. If both were held in trust, as a means of doing good, how different would be the result! For this reason, I should never wish children to learn anything because some of their companions were learning it. I would always offer present or future *usefulness* as a motive. For instance, if a daughter were very desirous of learning music, I would ask her *why* she desired it. If she answered, or if I had reason to think, it was because some one else was learning it, I would at once discountenance it, by telling her the motive was a very poor one; but if she said she wished too learn, because she loved it very much, I would readily enter into her wishes, and promise to ask her father's permission. If the request were granted, I would say, 'You know we are not rich enough to have good music-masters for all of you; but your father is willing to expend more upon you than he could otherwise afford, from the idea that you will learn carefully and thoroughly, and thus be able to teach your brothers and sisters. At some future time your music may perhaps be the means of supporting yourself and doing good to others. You can likewise bring it into immediate use; for you will very soon be able to amuse your father in return for this kind indulgence.'

I have known young ladies, on whom a good deal had been expended, who more than repaid their parents by their assistance in educating younger branches of the family; and is not such a preparation likely to make the duties of a mother more pleasant and familiar to them? In some cases the acquirements and industry of one branch of the family have served to educate and bring forward all the rest; is not such a power, well-used, extremely conducive to kindness and benevolence?

It is certainly very desirable to fit children for the station they are likely to fill, as far as a parent can judge what that station will be. In this country, it is a difficult point to decide; for half our people are in a totally different situation from what might have been expected in their childhood. However, one maxim is as safe as it is true—i. e. A well informed mind is the happiest and the most useful in all situations. Every new acquirement is something added to a solid capital. To imitate every passing fashion is a very different thing from gaining knowledge. To thrum a few tunes upon a piano, and paint a few gaudy flowers, does not deserve to be spoken of as a part of *education*;—a fashionable scarf, or a bright ribbon, might as well be called so. I would never have music, painting, &c., learned at all, unless they could be learned perfectly, and practised with real good taste; and here I would make the passing remark, that a well-cultivated, *observing* mind, is most likely to be tasteful in all the lighter and more ornamental branches. The sure way to succeed in anything is to cultivate the intellectual faculties, and keep the powers of attention wide awake. If the mental faculties are kept vigorous by constant use, they will excel in anything to which their strength is applied. I think it is peculiarly unwise to sacrifice comfort, benevolence, or the more solid branches of learning, to any of the elegant arts; but when you can attain all these and a little more, it is much better to spend the surplus in giving your children a new pleasure, and an additional resource against poverty, than it is to expend it in superfluous articles of dress, or furniture. The same remarks that apply to music, drawing, &c., apply to a variety of things, that may be acquired at little or no expence—such as braiding straw, working muslin, doing rug-work, &c.—I would teach a child to learn every innocent thing, which it is in her power to learn. If it is not wanted immediately, it can be laid by for future use. I have a strong partiality for those old-fashioned employments, marking and rug-work. The formation of the figures, counting the threads, and arranging the colors, require a great deal of care; and the necessity of close attention is extremely salutary to young people.

Important as a love of reading is, there are cases where it ought to be checked. It is mere selfishness and indolence to neglect active duties for the sake of books; we have no right to do it. Children of a languid and lazy temperament are sometimes willing to devote all their time to reading, for the sake of avoiding bodily exertion; such a tendency should be counteracted by endeavoring to interest them in active duties and amusements. 'Particular pains should be taken to induce them to attend to the feelings of others. Whatever services and attentions they exact from others, they should be obliged in their turn to pay.' Out of door exercise, frequent walks, and a lively attention to the beauties of nature, are very beneficial to such dispositions. On the contrary, those who have no love for quiet, mental pleasures, should be attracted by interesting books and entertaining conversation. A mother needs to be something of a philosopher.—In other, and better words, she needs a great deal of practical good sense, and habits of close observation.

With regard to what is called a *natural genius* for any particular employment, I think it should be fostered, wherever it is decidedly shown; but great care should be taken to distinguish between a strong natural bias and the sudden whims and caprices, to which companions, or accidental circumstances, have given birth. No doubt each individual has the gift to do some one particular thing better than others, if he could but discover what that gift is. We all do best what we strongly love to do. I believe the perfect and entire union of duty and inclination in our employments constitutes genius. Men seldom become very great in any pursuit they do not love with the whole heart and soul; and since this is the way to arrive at the greatest perfection, it is very desirable to find out the bias of character in early life. This is not to be done by asking questions; but by quietly observing what a child most delights in, and what he asks about most frequently and eagerly.

With regard to lessons, reading, and work, the attention of children should be kept awake by talking with them, asking questions on the subject, and showing them the best and most convenient methods of doing whatever they are about; but great care should be taken not to help them too much. No more assistance than is absolutely necessary should be given.—Leave them to their own ingenuity. Young people will always be helpless, if they are not obliged to think and do for themselves.

With regard to the kind of books that are read, great precaution should be used. No doubt the destiny of individuals has very often been decided by volumes accidentally picked up and eagerly devoured at a period of life when every new impression is powerful and abiding. For this reason, parents, or some guardian friends, should carefully examine every volume they put into the hands of young people. In doing this, the disposition and character of the child should be considered. If a bold, ambitious boy is dazzled by the trappings of war, and you do not wish to indulge his disposition to be a soldier, avoid placing in his way fascinating biographies of military heroes; for the same reason do not strengthen a restless, roving tendency by accounts of remarkable voyages and adventures. I do not mean to speak disparagingly of Voyages and Travels; I consider them the best and most attractive books in the world; I merely suggest a caution against strengthening any dangerous bias of character.

A calm, steady temperament may be safely indulged in reading works of imagination,—nay, perhaps requires such excitement to rouse it sufficiently,—but an excitable, romantic disposition should be indulged sparingly in such reading. To forbid all works of fiction cannot do good. There is an age when all mortals, of any sense or feeling, are naturally romantic and imaginative. This state of feeling, instead of being violently wrestled with, should be carefully guided and restrained, by reading only the purest and most eloquent works of fiction. The admirable and unfortunate Lady Russell, in a letter, written on the anniversary of her husband's execution, says, 'At such seasons I do not *contend* with

frail nature, but *keep her as innocent as I can.*'   This
rule may be wisely applied to that period of life when
young people, from the excess of mental energy, and
the riot of unwearied fancy, are most bewitched to read
novels.

Never countenance by word or example that silly
affected sensibility which leads people to faint or run
away at the sight of danger or distress.   If such a
habit is formed, try to conquer it by reasoning, and by
direct appeals to good feeling.   Nothing can be more
selfish than to run away from those who are suffering,
merely because the sight is painful.   True sensibility
leads us to overcome our own feelings for the good of
others.

Great caution should be used with regard to the
habits of talking in a family.   Talk of *things* rather
than of *persons*, lest your children early imbibe a love
of gossipping.   Particularly avoid the habit of speaking
ill of others.   We acquire great quickness of perception
in those things to which we give attention in early life ;
and if we have been in the habit of dwelling on the
defects of others, we shall not only be ill-natured in our
feelings, but we shall actually have the faculty of perceiving blemishes much more readily than virtues.
This tendency always to look on the black side is a
very unfortunate habit, and may often be traced to the
influences around us in childhood.

Some people fly to the opposite extreme.   From
the idea of being charitable, they gloss over everything,
and make no distinction between vice and virtue.   This
is false charity.   We should not speak well of what we
do not believe to be good and true.   We may avoid

saying anything of persons, unless we can speak well of
them; but when we are *obliged* to discuss a subject,
we should never in the least degree palliate and excuse
what we know to be wrong.

It is a great mistake to think that education is *finished* when young people leave school. Education is
never finished. Half the character is formed after we
cease to learn lessons from books; and at that active
and eager age it is formed with a rapidity and strength
absolutely startling to think of. Do you ask what forms
it? I answer the every-day conversation they hear, the
habits they witness, and the people they are taught to
respect. Sentiments thrown out in jest, or carelessness,
and perhaps forgotten by the speaker as soon as uttered, often sink deeply into the youthful mind, and
have a powerful influence on future character. This
is true in very early childhood; and it is peculiarly true
at the period when youth is just ripening into manhood.
Employ what teachers we may, the influences at home
will have the mightiest influences in education. School-
masters may cultivate the *intellect;* but the things said
and done at home are busy agents in forming the *affections;* and the latter have infinitely more important
consequences than the former.

A knowledge of domestic duties is beyond all price
to a woman. Every one ought to know how to sew,
and knit, and mend, and cook, and superintend a household. In every situation of life, high or low, this sort
of knowledge is a great advantage. There is no necessity that the gaining of such information should interfere with intellectual acquirement, or even with elegant
accomplishments. A well regulated mind can find time

to attend to all. When a girl is nine or ten years old, she should be accustomed to take some regular share in household duties, and to feel responsible for the manner in which it is done,—such as doing her own mending and making, washing the cups and putting them in place, cleaning the silver, dusting the parlor, &c. This should not be done occasionally, and neglected whenever she finds it convenient; she should consider it her department. When they are older than twelve, girls should begin to take turns in superintending the household, keeping an account of weekly expenses, cooking puddings, pies, cake, &c. To learn anything effectually, they should actually do these things themselves,— not stand by, and see others do them. It is a great mistake in mothers to make such slaves of themselves, rather than divide their cares with daughters. A variety of employment, and a feeling of trust and responsibility, add very much to the real happiness of young people. All who have observed human nature closely will agree that a vast deal depends upon how people deport themselves the first year after their marriage. If any little dissensions arise during that period,—if fretfulness and repining be indulged on one side, indifference and dislike on the other will surely follow,—and when this once takes place, farewell to all hopes of perfect domestic love. People may indeed agree to live peaceably and respectably together,—but the charm is broken— the best and dearest gift God gives to mortals is lost. Nothing can ever supply the place of that spontaneous tenderness, that boundless sympathy of soul, which has been so thoughtlessly destroyed. 'Beware of the first quarrel,' is the best advice that was ever given to mar-

14

ried people. Now I would ask any reflecting mother, whether a girl brought up in ignorance of household duties, is not very likely to fret, when she is first obliged to attend to them? Will not her want of practice decidedly interfere with the domestic comfort of her family, and will it not likewise be a very serious trial to her own temper? I have known many instances where young married women have been perplexed, discouraged, and miserable, under a sense of domestic cares, which, being so entirely new to them, seemed absolutely insupportable. The spirit of complaint to which this naturally gives rise is not very complimentary to the husband; and it is not wonderful if he becomes dissatisfied with a wife, whom he cannot render happy.

Young girls learn many mischievous lessons from their companions at school. Among a mass of young ladies collected from all sorts of families, there will of course be much vanity, frivolity, and deceit, and some indecency. The utmost watchfulness of a teacher cannot prevent some bad influences. For this reason, I should myself decidedly prefer instructing a daughter in my own house; but I am aware that in most families this course would be expensive and inconvenient. However, I would never trust a young girl at a boarding school without being sure that her room-mate was discreet, well-principled, and candid. I should rather have a daughter's mind a little less improved, than to have her heart exposed to corrupt influences; for this reason, I should prefer a respectable school in the country to a fashionable one in the city. For the same reason, I should greatly dread a young lady's making long visits from home, unless I had perfect confidence in every member of the family she visited, and in every person to whom they would be likely to introduce her. There is no calculating the mischief that is done by the chance acquaintances picked up in this way. If there are sons in the families visited, the danger is still greater. I do not, of course, allude to any immorality of conduct; I should hope girls even tolerably educated would never be guilty of anything like immodesty. But young ladies, ignorant of the world and its vices, often do imprudent things without knowing them to be imprudent. If they have strong and enthusiastic affections, even their innocent frankness will in all probability be misconstrued by those who are not themselves pure and open-hearted. At all events, the frequent intercourse likely to exist between a visitor and the brothers of her friend is extremely apt to fill her head with a diseased anxiety for the admiration of the other sex, and with silly, romantic ideas about love—ideas which have no foundation in reason, nature, or common sense. Many unhappy matches have been the result of placing young people under the influence of such sentimental excitement, before they were old enough to know their own minds. Such unions are often dignified with the name of *love*-matches; but love has nothing to do with the business—fancy, vanity, or passion is the agent; and vanity is by far the most busy of the three. To call such thoughtless connexions *love*-matches is a libel upon the deepest, holiest, and most thoughtful of all the passions.

In this country, girls are often left to themselves at the very period when, above all others, they need a mother's care. In France, mothers always visit with their daughters; and if restraint upon unmarried people is carried to excess there, we certainly err on the opposite extreme. We allow too much freedom, and we allow it too soon. I believe it is much better for a very young lady never to go about alone, or visit for any length of time from home, without her mother.

Youth must have friends, and those friends, being loved ardently, will have prodigious influence. The choice requires extreme caution. The whole of human destiny is often materially affected by those with whom we are intimate at fourteen or fifteen years of age. The safest method is not to put children in the way of those whom you dare not trust. Do not expressly forbid an acquaintance, (unless great faults of character demand such restrictions,) but endeavor by every possible means to withdraw your child from society you deem improper; occupy her with other things, and interest her in other persons. If an intimacy does spring up, notwithstanding your precautions, talk openly and reasonably about it; and let your daughter understand that you decidedly object to something in the young lady's principles, manners, or habits. Wealth and station should never be spoken of as either for or against forming a friendship; the generous mind of youth never thinks of these artificial distinctions, and we certainly do wrong to teach them. Your chief safety lies in the manner in which you have educated your daughter. If her mind, heart, and conscience have all been cultivated, she will not love to associate with the ignorant, the vulgar, and the vicious; she will naturally seek the well-informed, the well-principled, and the truly refined, because she will have most sympathy with them.

A mother has an undoubted right to inspect her children's letters, as well as the books they read; and if a young lady feels this to be any hardship, there is certainly something wrong, in one or other of the parties. Where young people are habitually discreet, it is not well to exercise this right very often; but children should always feel perfectly willing that letters may be opened, or not, at a parent's option. But parents, on their part, must consider that this entire confidence cannot naturally and reasonably be expected to exist, unless they evince perfect good-nature, and a lively sympathy with youthful feeling. Perfect confidence between parent and child is a seven-fold shield against temptation.

There is one subject, on which I am very anxious to say a great deal; but on which, for obvious reasons, I can say very little. Judging by my own observation, I believe it to be the greatest evil now existing in education. I mean the want of confidence between mothers and daughters on delicate subjects. Children, from books, and from their own observation, soon have their curiosity excited on such subjects; this is perfectly natural and innocent, and if frankly met by a mother, it would never do harm. But on these occasions it is customary either to put young people off with lies, or still further to excite their curiosity by mystery and embarrassment. Information being refused them at the only proper source, they immediately have recourse to domestics, or immodest school-companions; and very often their young minds are polluted with filthy

14 *

anecdotes of vice and vulgarity. This ought not to be. Mothers are the only proper persons to convey such knowledge to a child's mind. They can do it without throwing the slightest stain upon youthful purity ; and it is an imperious duty that they should do it. A girl who receives her first ideas on these subjects from the shameless stories and indecent jokes of vulgar associates, has in fact prostituted her mind by familiarity with vice. A diseased curiosity is excited, and undue importance given to subjects, which those she has been taught to respect think it necessary to envelope in so much mystery ; she learns to think a great deal about them, and to ask a great many questions. This does not spring from any natural impurity ; the same restless curiosity would be excited by any subject treated in the same manner. On the contrary, a well-educated girl of twelve years old, would be perfectly satisfied with a frank, rational explanation from a mother. It would set her mind at rest upon the subject ; and instinctive modesty would prevent her recurring to it unnecessarily, or making it a theme of conversation with others. Mothers are strangely averse to encouraging this sort of confidence. I know not why it is, but they are usually the very last persons in the world to whom daughters think of applying in these cases. Many a young lady has fallen a victim to consumption from a mother's bashfulness in imparting necessary precautions ; and many, oh, many more, have had their minds corrupted beyond all cure.

I would not by any means be understood to approve of frequent conversations of this kind between parent and child—and least of all, anything like jesting, or double meanings. I never saw but two women, who indulged in such kind of mirth before their daughters; and I never think of them but with unmingled disgust. I do believe that after one modest and rational explanation, the natural purity and timidity of youth would check a disposition to talk much about it.

It is usually thought necessary, even by the very conscientious, to tell falsehoods about such subjects; but I believe it cannot do good, and may do harm. I would say to a young child, 'I cannot tell you now, because you are not old enough to understand it. When you are old enough, I will talk with you; but you must remember not to ask anybody but me. You know I always have a reason for what I say to you; and I tell you it would be very improper to talk with other people about it. I promise you that I will explain it all to you, as soon as you are old enough to understand it.'

This promise ought to be faithfully kept; and if young people meet with anything in books that requires explanation, they should be taught to apply to their mother, and to no one else. Such a course would, I am very sure, prevent a great deal of impurity and imprudence.

It is a bad plan for young girls to sleep with nursery maids, unless you have the utmost confidence in the good principles and modesty of your domestics. There is a strong love among vulgar people of telling secrets, and talking on forbidden subjects. From a large proportion of domestics this danger is so great, that I apprehend a prudent mother will very rarely, under any circumstances, place her daughter in the same sleeping apartment with a domestic, until her character is so much formed, that her own dignity will lead her to reject all improper conversation. A well-principled, amiable elder sister is a great safeguard to a girl's purity of thought and propriety of behavior. It is extremely important that warm-hearted, imprudent youth, should have a safe and interesting companion. A judicious mother can do a vast deal toward supplying this want; but those who have such a shield as a good sister are doubly blessed.

In the chapter on politeness I have mentioned how much little courtesies and kind attentions tend to strengthen the bonds of family love; and I firmly believe that these things, small as they may appear singly and separately, are of very great importance. Everything which ties the heart to home, has a good influence. Brothers and sisters cannot be too much encouraged in perfect kindness and candor toward each other. Any slight rudeness, a want of consideration for each other's feelings, or of attention to each other's comfort, should be treated with quite as much importance as similar offences against strangers. The habit of putting on politeness to go abroad, and of throwing it off at home, does more moral mischief than we are apt to imagine. I know families, conscientious in all *great* things, who yet think it no harm to peep into each other's letters, or use each other's property without permission; yet I look upon these things as absolutely unprincipled; they are positive infringements of the golden rule.

If one member of a family have any peculiarity, or personal defect, he should be treated with unusual delicacy and affection. The best way to cure any defect is to treat persons in such a manner, that they them-

selves forget it. Perpetual consciousness of any disagreeable peculiarity increases the evil prodigiously. This
is particularly true of physical imperfections; stuttering
and lisping, for instance, are made ten times worse by
being laughed at, or observed. It is the fear of exciting
remark that makes people stutter so much worse before
strangers than in the presence of their friends.

Parents are too apt to show a preference for the
smartest or prettiest of the family. This is exactly the
reverse of right. Those who are the least attractive
abroad should be the most fostered at home; otherwise
they may become chilled and discouraged; and the
talents and good qualities they have, may die away in
the secrecy of their own bosoms, for want of something
to call them into exercise.

The business of parents is to develope each individual
character so as to produce the greatest amount of usefulness and happiness. It is very selfish to bestow the
most attention upon those who are the most pleasing,
or most likely to do credit to a parent in the eyes of
the world. Those who are painfully diffident of themselves should be treated with distinguished regard; they
should be consulted on interesting subjects, and when
their opinions are injudicious, they should be met by
open and manly arguments, and never treated with any
degree of contempt or indifference.

To have the various members of a family feel a
common interest, as if they were all portions of the
same body, is extremely desirable. It is a beautiful
sight to see sisters willing to devote their talents and
industry to the education of brothers, or a brother willing
to deny himself selfish gratifications for a sister's improve-

ment, or a parent's comfort.   Little respectful attentions
to a parent tend very much to produce this delightful
domestic sympathy.   Nothing is more graceful than
children employed in placing a father's arm-chair and
slippers, or busying themselves in making everything
look cheerful against his return; and there is something
more than mere looks concerned in these becoming
attentions—these trifling things lay the foundation of
strong and deeply virtuous feelings.   The vices and
temptations of the world have little danger for those
who can recollect beloved parents and a happy home.
The holy and purifying influence is carried through life,
and descends to bless and encourage succeeding genera-
tions.   For this reason, too much cannot be done to
produce an earnest and confiding friendship between
parents and children.   Mothers should take every
opportunity to excite love, gratitude and respect, toward
a father.   His virtues and his kindness should be a favorite
theme, when talking with his children.   The same rule
that applies to a wife, in these respects, of course applies
to a husband.   It should be the business of each to
strengthen the bonds of domestic union.

Every effort should be made to make home as pleasant as possible.   The habit of taking turns to read
interesting books aloud, while the others are at work,
is an excellent plan.   Music has likewise a cheerful
influence, and greatly tends to produce refinement of
taste.   It has a very salutary effect for whole families
to unite in singing before retiring to rest; or at any
other time, when it is pleasant and convenient.   On
such occasions, I think there should be at least one
simple tune in which the little children can join without

injury to their young voices. I believe the power of learning to sing is much more general than has hitherto been believed; and the more subjects there are in which the different members of a family can sympathize, the greater will be their harmony and love.

It will probably be gathered from what I have said in the preceding pages, that I do not approve of young ladies' visiting very young,—that is, being what is called *brought out*, or *going into company*. I think those parents whose situation does not make it necessary to have their daughters *brought out* at all, are peculiarly blest; and under all circumstances, I am sure it is best for a daughter never to visit without her mother, till she is past seventeen years of age. A round of gayety is alike fascinating and unprofitable; it wastes time, distracts attention. and makes every-day duties and pleasures appear dull and uninteresting. Late hours, excitement, and irregularity of food, make large demands upon health and strength, before the constitution is fully established; the mind and heart too, as well as the body, become old before their time; there is nothing new in store for the young imagination, and society loses its charm at the very age when it would naturally be most enjoyed. I do not believe it is *ever* well for girls to go into many large parties; the manners can be sufficiently formed by social intercourse with the polite and intelligent. I greatly approve of social visiting among children and young persons. It is alike beneficial to the heart. and the manners. I only wish that mothers more generally *made one* of these little parties. In general, girls think they must have an apartment to themselves when they receive visiters, or they must run off into the garden, or upstairs, because a mother's presence is an unpleasant restraint. This ought not to be. If married ladies will be familiar and cheerful, they can be extremely entertaining, as well as useful to the young. I wish this sort of companionship were more general—for I am certain it has a good influence. If a mother shows an obliging readiness to enter into the plans and amusements of her children, and their young guests, they will feel no painful restraint in her presence; while at the same time she removes from them all temptation to frivolous and improper conversation. I have known instances where a mother was the most animated and animating of all the little group. Would such instances were more frequent! It is impossible to calculate the benefits that result from having a *happy home.*

From the beginning to the end of this book, I have most earnestly represented the necessity of forming early habits of observation. It is a strong foundation, on which any kind of character may be built, as circumstances require. It makes good writers, good painters, good botanists, good mechanics, good cooks, good housewives, good farmers—good everything! It fits us for any situation in which Providence may place us, and enables us to make the most of whatever advantages may come in our way. It is a sort of vital principle, that gives life to everything.

Not fifty miles from Boston is a farmer, quite famous for the improvements he has made in the wild grape. He found a vine in the wood, which dozens of his neighbors passed every week, as well as he; but he *observed* that where the oxen fed upon the vine the grapes where largest and sweetest. He took the hint.

The vine was transplanted, and closely pruned. This produced the same effect as browsing had done; the nourishment, that in a wild state supported a great weight of vines and tendrils, went entirely to the body of the grape. His neighbors would have known this as well as he, if they had thought about it; but they did not *observe*.

In ancient Greece the beneficial effect of closely trimming grape-vines was discovered by *observing* the extreme luxuriance of a vine, which an ass had frequently nibbled as he fed by the way-side. The man who availed himself of this hint, became celebrated throughout Greece, by means of the far-famed grapes of Nauplia; and, with less justice, statues were erected to the ass, and high honors paid to his memory. The grape had never been cultivated in this country, when, by a singular coincidence, an observing American farmer made the same discovery, and by the same means, that gave celebrity to the observing Grecian farmer, in very ancient times.

Even in infancy, the foundation of this important habit should be begun, by directing the attention to the size, shape, color, &c., of whatever objects are presented. In childhood it should be constantly kept alive, by never allowing anything to be read, or done, carelessly; and during the teens, when the mind is all alive and busy, very peculiar care should be taken to strengthen and confirm it. A young lady should never be satisfied with getting through with a thing some how or other; she should know *how* she has done it, *why* she has done it, and what is the *best way* of doing it. She should use her thoughts in all her employments. There is

15

always a best way of doing everything; and however trifling the occupation, this way should be discovered; in making a shirt, for instance, she should be led to observe that it is much more convenient to put in the sleeves before the collar is set on. It is the want of these habits of observation, which makes some people so left-handed and awkward about everything they undertake.

There is another subject quite as important—I mean *habits of reflection*. Young people should be accustomed to look into their own hearts, to be very sure what motives they act from, and what feelings they indulge. Parents can assist them very much, by seizing favorable opportunities to talk with them about what they have done, and what were their motives of action. It is a good maxim 'every morning to think what we have to do, and every evening to think what we have done.' The close of the year is a peculiarly appropriate time for self-examination. Each member of the family should be encouraged at this interesting season, to think what improvements have been made, and what evils have been conquered during the year.

*　　*　　*　　*　　*　　*

One subject of great importance had nearly escaped my recollection. I mean the early habit of writing letters neatly and correctly. There are a hundred cases where a young person's success in life may be affected by the appearance of their epistles. A letter badly written, badly spelt, or badly punctuated, is a direct and abiding proof of a neglected education, or a disorderly mind. The receipt of such a document often makes an unfavorable impression with regard to an individual's character, or capacity, which is never afterward entirely obliterated. For this reason, children should early be accustomed to give a natural and simple account, in writing, of what they have seen and done. The rules of punctuation, which are few and plain, should be particularly attended to; and any awkwardness or inelegance in the sentences should be kindly pointed out, but never ridiculed. If parents, from want of early education, feel unable to do this, they will, in all probability, know of some near relation, or intimate friend, who will occasionally attend to it. The great thing is to make children *desirous* of improvement; and this can be done by an uneducated parent, as well as by a learned one. When a strong *wish* to excel in any particular thing is once excited, there is no danger but it will find means to satisfy itself; and this is one reason why we should be more careful what we teach children to *love*, than what we teach them to *remember*.

CHAPTER XI.

VIEWS OF MATRIMONY.

THERE is no subject connected with education which has so important a bearing on human happiness as the views young people are taught to entertain with regard to matrimonial connexions. The dreams of silly romance, half vanity, and half passion, on the one hand, and selfish calculation on the other, leave but precious

little of just thinking and right feeling on the subject.
The greatest and most prevailing error in education
consists in making lovers a subject of such engrossing
and disproportionate interest in the minds of young
girls. As soon as they can walk alone, they are called
'little sweet-heart,' and 'little wife;' as they grow older,
the boyish liking of a neighbor, or school-mate, becomes
a favorite jest; they often hear it said how lucky such
and such people are, because they '*married off*' all
their family so young; and when a pretty, attractive girl
is mentioned, they are in the habit of hearing it observed, 'She will be married young. She is too handsome
and too interesting to live single long.'

I have frequently said that such sort of accidental
remarks do in fact *educate* children, more than direct
maxims; and this applies with peculiar force to the subject of matrimony. Such observations as I have quoted,
give young girls the idea that there is something degrading in not being married young; or, at least, in not having
had offers of marriage. This induces a kind of silly
pride and restless vanity, which too often ends in ill-
assorted connexions. I had a sweet young friend,
with a most warm and generous heart, but a giddy, romantic brain. Her mother was weak-minded and indulgent, and had herself been taught, in early life, to
consider it the chief end and aim of existence to get
married. She often reminded her daughters, that she
was but sixteen when she was married, and had then
refused two or three lovers. Of course, when my
charming, sentimental little friend was sixteen, she began
to feel uneasy under a sense of disgrace; her pride was
concerned in having a beau as early as her mother had

one; and this feeling was a good deal strengthened by the engagement of two or three young companions. It unluckily happened that a dashing, worthless young man was introduced to her about this time. A flirtation began, which soon ended in an offer of his hand. He said he was in good business, and she saw that he wore a hand-some coat, and drove a superb horse; and, more than all, she thought what a triumph it would be to be en-gaged at sixteen. She married him. It was soon dis-covered that he was careless, dissipated, and very poor. In no respect whatever had he sympathy with my sen-sitive, refined, but ill-educated friend. She discovered this too late. She would have discovered it at first, had her mind been *quiet* on the subject of matrimony. A wretched life might have been spared her, if her mother had left her heart to develope naturally, under the in-fluences of true affection, as the lily opens its petals to the sunshine. Her marriage was called a *love-match;* and as such was held up by ambitious parents as a salu-tary warning. But there never was a greater misnomer. She had not a particle of love for the man. She mar-ried him because he happened to be the first that offered, and because she felt ashamed not to be engaged as soon as her companions.

But heedless vanity and silly romance, though a prolific source of unhappy marriages, are not so disastrous in their effects as worldly ambition, and selfish calculation. I never knew a marriage ex-pressly for money, that did not end unhappily. Yet managing mothers, and heartless daughters, are contin-ually playing the same unlucky game. I look upon it as something more than bad policy for people to marry

15 *

those to whom they are, at best, perfectly indifferent,
merely for the sake of wealth; in my view it is absolutely unprincipled. Happiness cannot result from such
connexions, because it ought not. A mother who can
deliberately advise a daughter thus to throw away all
chance of domestic bliss, would, were it not for the
fear of public opinion, be willing to sell her to the
Grand Sultan, to grace his seraglio. Disguise the matter as we may, with the softening epithets of 'prudent
match,' 'a good establishment,' &c., it is, in honest truth,
a matter of bargain and sale.

I believe men more frequently marry for love, than
women; because they have a freer choice. I am
afraid to conjecture how large a proportion of women
marry because they think they shall not have a better
chance, and dread being dependent. Such marriages,
no doubt, sometimes prove tolerably comfortable; but
great numbers would have been far happier single. If
I may judge by my own observation of such matches,
marrying for a home is a most tiresome way of getting
a living.

One of the worst effects resulting from *managing*
about these things, is the disappointment and fan-
cied disgrace attendant upon a failure; and with the
most artful manœuvring, failures in such schemes are
very frequent. Human policy sketches beautiful pat-
terns, but she is a bad weaver; she always entangles
her own web. I am acquainted with two or three managing mothers, who have pretty children; and in the
whole circle of my acquaintance, I know of none so
unfortunate in disposing of their daughters. The young
ladies would have married very well, if they had not

been taught to act a part; now, they will either live single, or form ill-assorted, unhappy connexions. If they live single, they will probably be ill-natured and envious through life; because they have been taught to attach so much importance to the mere circumstance of getting married, without any reference to genuine affection. A woman of well-regulated feelings and an active mind, may be very happy in single life,—far happier than she could be made by a marriage of expediency. The reason old maids are proverbially more discontented than old bachelors, is, that they have generally so much less to occupy their thoughts. For this reason, it is peculiarly important, that a woman's education should furnish her with abundant resources for employment and amusement. I do not say that an unmarried woman can be as happy as one who forms, with proper views and feelings, a union, which is unquestionably the most blessed of all human relations; but I am very certain that one properly educated need not be unhappy in single life.

The great difficulty at the present day is, that matrimony is made a subject of pride, vanity, or expediency; whereas it ought to be a matter of free choice and honest preference. A woman educated with proper views on the subject could not be excessively troubled at not being married, when in fact she had never seen a person for whom she entertained particular affection; but one taught to regard it as a matter of pride, is inevitably wretched, discontented, and envious, under the prospect of being an old maid, though she regards no human being with anything like love.

Some mothers are always talking about the cares, and duties, and sacrifices incident to married life; they are always urging their daughters to 'enjoy themselves while they are single'—'to be happy while they have a chance,'—but at the same time that they give such a gloomy picture of domestic life, (making it a frightful bugbear to the young imagination,) they urge upon them the necessity of getting married for respectability's sake. They *must* be 'well settled,' as the phrase is. The victim must be sacrificed, because the world's opinion demands it.

I once heard a girl, accustomed to such remarks, say, with apparent sincerity, 'I should like of all things to be married, if I could be sure my husband would die in a fortnight; then I should avoid the *disgrace* of being an old maid, and get rid of the restraint and trouble of married life.' Strange and unnatural as such a sentiment may appear, it was just what might have been expected from one accustomed to such selfish views of a relation so holy and blessed in its nature. It is all-important that charming pictures of domestic life should be presented to the young. It should be described as,—what it really is,—the home of woman's affections, and her pleasantest sphere of duty. Your daughter should never hear her own marriage speculated or jested upon; but the subject in general should be associated in her mind with everything pure, bright, and cheerful.

I shall be asked if I do not think it extremely desirable that daughters should marry well; and whether the secluded, domestic education I have recommended is not very unfavorable to the completion of such wishes,

—for how can they be admired, when they are not seen? It certainly is very desirable that daughters should marry well, because it wonderfully increases their chance of happiness. The unchangeable laws of God have made reciprocated affection necessary to the human heart; and marriage formed with proper views is a powerful means of improving our better nature. But I would not say, or do anything, to promote a union of this sort. I would have no scheming, no managing, no hinting. I would never talk with girls about the beaux, or suffer them to associate with those who did. I would leave everything to nature and Divine Providence—with a full belief that such reliance would do more and better for me than I could effect by my own plans. I do not think a secluded, domestic education is unfavorable to chances of happy matrimonial connexions. A girl with a good heart, a full mind, and modest, refined manners, cannot fail to be attractive. Make her a delightful companion to her own family; teach her to be happy at home; and trust Divine Providence to find her a suitable partner. If she has been taught to think the regulation of her own heart and mind of greater importance than anything else, she cannot be unhappy whatever may be her lot in life; and her chance for a happy marriage will be abundantly greater than it could be made by the most adroit management.

It is evident that the greatest safeguard against improper attachments consists in the character you have given your daughter, by the manner of educating her. A refined young lady will not naturally be in love with vulgarity; nor will a pure mind have any sympathy with the vicious and unprincipled. But as vice often wears the garb of virtue, and as youth is, from its very innocence, unsuspecting, it is incumbent upon parents to be extremely careful with what sort of young men they allow their daughters to associate. Acquaintance with any particular person should not be expressly forbidden, because such restraint is likely to excite the very interest you wish to avoid; but, without saying anything on the subject, do not encourage your daughter in going to places where she will meet a fascinating young man, to whom you have decided objections; and if you discover the smallest symptoms of mutual interest between the parties, remove her from home, if possible, to some place where her mind will soon become interested in new occupations. A prudent parent will always remember that it is extremely natural for young people to get deeply interested in those they see frequently; and that it is far easier, and better, to prevent an attachment, than it is to conquer it after it is formed. I would never, even by the most trifling expression, lead my daughter to think of her acquaintances as future lovers; but I should myself recollect the possibility of such a circumstance, and would not therefore encourage an acquaintance with any man, whom I should be very unwilling to see her husband. 'An ounce of prevention is worth a pound of cure.'

In affairs of this kind strong opposition is very impolitic. It rarely effects its purpose; and if it does, it is through much misery and trouble. I doubt whether parents have a right to forbid the marriage of their children, after they are old enough to think and decide for themselves; but while they are quite young, I do think they have an undoubted right to prevent marriage, until the laws of the land render them free from parental authority.   But where this is done, it should be with great mildness and discretion : it should be resorted to only from a desire to leave young people a perfect freedom of choice, at an age when they are more capable of feeling deeply and judging wisely.

Where there is any immorality of character, it becomes an imperative duty for parents to forbid an engagement while the parties are young.   If it is persisted in, after they are old enough to be as discreet as they ever will be, there is no help for it; but I do not believe one, whose heart and mind had been properly educated, would ever persist in such a course.

The three great questions to be asked in deciding whether a union is suitable and desirable, is, 1st, Has the person good principles?   2d, Has he, or she, a good disposition?   3d, Is there a strong, decided, deeply-founded preference?   Connexions which are likely to lead a woman into a sphere of life to which she has been unaccustomed, to introduce her to new and arduous duties,—and to form a violent contrast to her previous mode of life,—should not be entered into, except at mature age, and with great certainty that affection is strong enough to endure such trials.   But where there is deep, well founded love, and an humble reliance on Divine Providence, all things will work right in the end.

APPLEWOOD BOOKS
BRINGING THE PAST ALIVE

*TIMELESS ADVICE & ENTERTAINMENT
FROM AMERICANS WHO CAME BEFORE US*

❦

*George Washington on Manners
Benjamin Franklin on Money
Lydia Maria Child on Raising Children
Henry David Thoreau on Walking*

&

Many More Distinctive Classics

Now Available Again

❦

At finer bookstores

& gift shops or from:

APPLEWOOD BOOKS
distributed by
The Globe Pequot Press
Box 833, Old Saybrook, CT 06475• (203) 526-9571